When Relationships Matter: Make Your Church A Place Where Kids & Teenagers Belong
Published by Orange, a division of The reThink Group, Inc.

5870 Charlotte Lane, Suite 300
Cumming, GA 30040 U.S.A.

The Orange logo is a registered trademark of The reThink Group, Inc.

All Scripture quotations, unless otherwise noted, are taken from the Holy Bible, New International Version®. NIV®. Copyright © 1973, 1978, 1984 by International Bible Society. Used by permission of Zondervan.

Other Orange products are available online and direct from the publisher.
Visit our website at www.ThinkOrange.com for more resources like these.

ISBN: 978-1-63570-093-0

©2019 The reThink Group, Inc.

Authors: Reggie Joiner, Kristen Ivy, Tom Shefchunas
Lead Editor: Afton Phillips
Editing Team: Afton Phillips, Adriana Howard, Laurin Greco, Lane Jones, Mike Jeffries
Design: Ryan Boon, FiveStone
Layout: Jacob Hunt
Project Manager: Nate Brandt

Printed in the United States of America

First Edition 2019

1 2 3 4 5 6 7 8 9 10

04/23/19

Copies of this book are available for distribution in churches, schools, and other venues at a significant quantity discount.
For more details, go to www.OrangeStore.org.

This book is based on conference presentations, training resources and Orange publicatons on creating a Lead Small Culture.

WHEN RELATIONSHIPS MATTER

Make Your Church a Place
Where Kids & Teenagers Belong

TABLE OF CONTENTS

INTRODUCTION 34

Give Kids Someone and Somewhere 8
Act Like You Believe it 24

IMPROVE YOUR STRUCTURE SO RELATIONSHIPS MATTER 34

Organize to be More Organic 44
Think Steps, Not Programs 58
Move to the Rhythm 74

EMPOWER LEADERS WHO MAKE RELATIONSHIPS MATTER 90

Expect More, Not Less 98
Play Favorites 112
Win Before You Begin 126

CREATE EXPERIENCES TO MAKE RELATIONSHIPS MATTER 140

Have Imaginary Conversations 148
Control the Climate 160
Measure What Seems Unmeasurable 172

CONCERTS, CLASSROOMS, CIRCLES 185

Do More Than A Concert 186
Drop Out Of Class 194
Transition To Circles 202

INTRODUCTION

These pages explore the values and practices that drive leaders who believe it's important to build a relationally driven model of church. It's specifically designed to help them create a church culture where small groups are a priority.

These leaders share a common conviction that kids and teenagers need other adults besides their parents.

They need other adults . . .
who believe in God.
who believe in them.
and who give them a place to belong.

That's why we wrote this book.

We're not claiming it answers every
question or solves every problem.

But it will give you more ideas on how to effectively establish
environments where kids can connect relationally.

If you want to influence what kids believe about God, themselves,
and the rest of the world, give them somewhere to belong.

That's why we also hope you will join this conversation
and champion the belief that relationships with kids
and teenagers should be a priority in our churches.

CHAPTER 1
GIVE KIDS SOMEONE AND SOMEWHERE

I love nouns. It's probably because nouns were the easiest things for me to identify when I (Reggie) had to diagram sentences for Miss McGuffey's class in high school. Nouns are simple. They're just a person, place, or thing. They're not nearly as confusing as adverbs, participles, or dangling modifiers. (Make sure you don't use that last term in front of middle schoolers.) I'm glad that nouns are clear, tangible, and concrete.

What does that have to do with creating a place for kids to belong? A lot. We think kids and teenagers need two important nouns in their life. They need *someone* and they need *somewhere*.

Before anyone can wrestle with abstract concepts like faith, hope, and the meaning of life, they simply need to know who loves them and where they belong. In my early days, I tried to hand students a list of action verbs before I handed them a few solid nouns. I think I forgot that in the English language, nouns usually come before verbs. Since then, I've learned that before you can expect kids to believe, you usually need to give them someone who believes in them. Before you ask teenagers to "go tell the world," you need to give them a safe place where they know they belong.

Kids need **two** important **nouns** so they can anchor their lives to something solid.
They need a *person*.
They need a *place*.

Research suggests the earlier they identify the "who"s and "where"s of their life, the more solid their faith. That's where you come in as a ministry leader. You can't force or determine the faith or future of anyone, really. The only thing you can actually do is recruit leaders and establish places so kids can know they belong somewhere.

Give Kids Someone.

Let's start with the "who." The premise of this book is that most kids need to belong before they can believe, or keep believing. That's why we think it's important to re-arrange your ministry to make sure kids and teenagers have people who know them and a place where they're known. We actually think a small group is one of the best ways to introduce this generation to the concept of a God who loves them unconditionally.

Think about it.

You can't see God.

I've never seen God, and neither have you.

Okay. Maybe you think you have. But I'm going to bet it wasn't actually God.

More than likely, you were staring too long at a cloud formation, or you drank too much Nyquil. The point is there are no tangible, verifiable images you can hold up and say, "This is God."

It's too bad social media didn't exist thousands of years ago. It would have settled a lot of issues for skeptics.

Imagine if . . .
Moses sent a pic of God writing the Ten Commandments.
Peter uploaded images of Jesus walking on the water.
John posted a video of Jesus ascending into heaven on YouTube.

(If social media had been around, it could have settled that whole dinosaur debate, too.)

Your job as a pastor or Christian leader would be a lot easier if those moments had been captured with some actual digital images.

Instead, you probably spend a lot of time trying to convince kids or teenagers to pursue a God they've never seen. It's tricky. God doesn't have an Instagram account or a Facebook page. So, how do you invite people to follow Someone they can't touch or see or hear? And how do you move them toward an authentic and personal faith in a God who may seem distant, vague, and unpredictable?

I (Reggie) have watched hundreds of churches debate which strategy is best for children and teenagers. I've listened to confident leaders promote their interpretation of Biblical truth and advocate their version of church as the solution for the dying faith of a generation. And while we all may not agree on every detail, we are connected by a common mission to help kids and adults grow in their relationship with Jesus Christ.

So, back to the question.
How do you build authentic faith in kids and teenagers?
We think we have finally discovered the answer.
And it's really simple.

Just kidding.

The truth is, it will never be simple. That's the nature of faith and pursuing a relationship with a mysterious and majestic Creator. We aren't writing this book because we think we have the answer, but because we've made a number of key observations through the years about kids and faith. Here are a few . . .

You don't shape a kid's faith by
teaching them doctrine.
(Whatever you talk them into, someone else can talk them out of.)

You don't shape a kid's faith by
persuading them to have better standards.
(They may ultimately give up if they feel like they can't measure up.)

You don't shape a kid's faith by
getting them to attend your events.
(At some point, they'll compare the quality of your production to what culture produces, and you'll probably lose.)

But you can shape a kid's faith by connecting them to caring adults who will be present in their life.

Are we saying theology, lifestyle, and church attendance don't matter? Not at all. But we *are* suggesting any of those things, without caring and consistent relationships, will have a limited impact. You don't have to look very far to find sobering stats about the number of teenagers and college students who have walked away from church.

Our experience suggests that most kids who grow up and leave church didn't run away from caring relationships. They ran away from . . .
prejudice
judgment
irrelevance
and religion.

RETHINK DISCIPLESHIP.

For the past twenty years, I (Reggie) have been able to hang out with a distinctive group of college students during the summer. They're the interns who show up to help at summer camps, and they represent a group of college-age individuals who didn't walk away from faith. Instead, they decided to use their summer breaks to invest in the faith of teenagers.

I'm always curious about their stories and what helped shape their faith to this point. At the beginning of the summer, I traditionally take them through an exercise. I ask them to pinpoint a few things in their past that contributed to their spiritual growth. Then, we write those things down on index cards, put them on a creative board, and look for similar patterns in their stories. For nearly two decades the results have been the same. Every defining moment in their stories always comes back to one or more of these five issues.

> *Life-changing truths* – change how they see themselves
>   or God
> *Spiritual disciplines* – help them connect personally to God
> *Ministry opportunities* – increase their sense of mission
> *Pivotal circumstances or events* – compel them to rethink
>   their priorities
> *Significant relationships* – help them navigate their
>   spiritual journey

One of the most enlightening moments of these sessions with our camp interns is always the point when we scan the board for the names of people who have impacted their lives. In everyone's story of faith, there are people who have shown up and become catalysts for their spiritual growth. Think about it. If you're reading this right now, chances are, you believe what you believe and you do what you do because of the way someone influenced your faith. More than likely, it wasn't just one person, but several. You could probably write down a short list of people who have been strategic influences in your life.

GOD USES PEOPLE.
Just like the people in ancient times developed their view of God as . . .
the God of Abraham,
the God of Isaac,
or the God of Moses,

You've developed a sense of who God is because you have met . . .
the God of Susan,
the God of Carlos,
or the God of Jeff.

God uses people. That's the point. He always has. Sometimes we forget the God of the Bible is the God of the people of the Bible. God has always used people to demonstrate His story of redemption.

The essence of our faith is linked to the idea that God actually became human. He became one of us.
So we could touch Him.
Hear Him.
See Him.

God simply decided the most effective way to redeem us was to become one of us.

The narrative of the Bible is anchored to the fact that God became a man so He could prove how much He loves us. And that Jesus literally became human. What happened on the cross and at the resurrection is so significant that sometimes we fail to recognize what God did just by showing up as a person.

He became us.
Not a book.
Not a really cuddly looking animal.
Not a supernatural being from Ezekiel's vision.
But a real, live, breathing human being.

So, what's the point of all of this? As believers, it's possible to get so caught up in our sermons, ordinances, doctrines, spiritual disciplines, and church programs that we forget the character of God was revealed to an ancient culture through an actual Person. Turn that one over in your head when you can't fall asleep at night. Evidently, God saw the need to show who He is to people who couldn't see Him by sending Someone they could see.

> **God saw the need to show who He is to people who couldn't see Him by sending Someone they could see.**

The incarnation is one of the most complicated paradoxical truths of our Christian faith. When Jesus came to Earth, Jesus was as much man as if He were not God at all, and as much God as if He were not man at all. He is God and man at the same time. He stepped onto the planet so we could see God. This is what makes our faith different from most other religions. We follow a Man who said He is God. He actually said things like, *"Anyone who has seen me has seen the Father."*[1] Of course, that statement raised a few eyebrows with the religious leaders. So they charged Him with blasphemy, convicted Him of a capital crime, and executed Him. The only problem: He is God, so He didn't stay dead.

Of course, because He is God, He accurately predicted He would be killed and then come back to life. For some reason, everyone was surprised when He actually did—but don't judge them too quickly. Sometimes it's just easier to understand things when we're looking backward. It kind of makes sense that what Jesus said before He died became a little clearer to the disciples after He came back to life.

When you read what Jesus says and you believe He actually came back to life, it gives His words a little extra punch. So, if you think something He said seems a little unreasonable or impossible, just remember—He was dead and now He's alive!

With that in mind, here's one of His statements that seems a little outlandish: *"Very truly I tell you, whoever believes in me will do the works I have been doing, and they will do even **greater** things than these, because I am going to the Father. . . . And I will ask the Father, and He will give you another advocate to help you and be with you forever—the Spirit of truth."*[2] Sounds a little crazy, doesn't it? When He left, Jesus promised to send His Spirit to be

---

1. John 14:9, NIV
2. John 14:12, 16-17a, NIV, emphasis added

here with us. Maybe that explains why He prayed such an unusual prayer, *"Father, just as you are in me and I am in you. May they [those who are followers of Jesus] also be in us* **so that the world may believe** *that you have sent me. . . .* **Then the world will know that you sent me and have loved them** *even as you have loved me."* [3]

Did you get it? Jesus, the God Man, the Man God, who died and rose again, predicted that one day the world will know He loves them, even though they can't see Him, because they can see the people who are following Him.

Please don't miss this.
People can't see God.
People can't see Jesus.
People can't see the Holy Spirit.

But people can see people who follow God.
People can see the Church.

That's why what you do, as a pastor or leader, is so important. The Church has been part of God's strategy for a long time. The best chance someone may have to personally see God is to get a close-up look at the people who follow God.

That's why your mission is simple, but complicated. You're supposed to do what Jesus did. Show up in the lives of others so they can see God. Engage with broken people so they can believe in the Jesus who bled for them. That's why the work of your church is so critical. You are called to do more than simply make a presentation of the Gospel. You are called to engage in the messiness of humanity because of the Gospel. You are compelled by the Spirit of Christ in you to convince your world that God

---

3. John 17:21b, 23b, NIV, emphasis added

loves them by the way you love them. The fact is, the Church is one of the most divinely strategic organizations that exists. But when or if a church fails to make relationships a priority, it risks becoming irrelevant.

> **The most valuable resources you have to help people see God are the people in your church who know God.**

So, let's settle it.
God wired your faith to be shaped and influenced by someone else's faith.
And God designed you to love people in such a way they can see Him working in you.

Regardless of the style or size of your church, your greatest asset to building faith in the next generation isn't your Bible study, worship band, facilities, or budget.

The most valuable resources you have to help people see God are the people in your church who know God.

And if you hope to help a generation of kids and teenagers know God, then you have to be strategic about how you connect them to small group leaders who believe in God and who believe in them.

When *Fortune* magazine named "The World's 50 Greatest Leaders," Geoffrey Canada was number twelve on the list. Canada has been someone we've respected for years because of his work with children and teenagers. A few years ago, we had the privilege of meeting with him. Canada is an education reformer who grew up in the South Bronx, went to Harvard graduate school, and came back to Harlem as the president and CEO of the Harlem Children's Zone. He has dedicated his life to giving disadvantaged kids a better chance by helping them graduate high school and get into college. In a conversation with Geoffrey, he made an interesting observation about the kids in Harlem. He said the reason so many of these kids don't believe in God is because they've never seen adults who are God-like. What he was saying was simple—in order to believe in a good and creative God who loves them in spite of their mistakes and their mess, kids and teenagers need adults who will do the same.

When relationships matter in your church, recruiting SGLs, or small group leaders, to invest weekly in the lives of kids will become the most important thing you do. We hope you're reading this book because you believe that, too. If you don't, we hope you will by the time you finish.

Our premise is simple.

Leaders who connect with kids in a SMALL group over time have the potential to make a BIG impact on their faith.

That's why we use the term **lead small**.

When you **lead small**, you simply make a choice to invest strategically in the lives of a few over time so you can help them build authentic faith.

When you **lead small**, you realize that what you do for a few will always have more potential than what you do for many.

So, if you want kids to know God, maybe one of the most important things you can do is to give them someone who will . . .
talk with them,
hang out with them,
do life with them.

The best way to help kids know God is to connect them with someone who knows God.

Give Kids Somewhere.

When relationships matter you tend to spend more time thinking about creating the right place to affect those relationships. Think of some of the best friendships you've observed. There was probably a significant gathering place that became the iconic symbol of the relationship.

Seinfeld had a diner.
Friends had a coffee house.
Cheers had a bar.
How I Met Your Mother had MacLaren's.
Blue Bloods had a big dining table.
Riverdale had Pop's.

Okay. Those may not be the best examples of relationships. But they all speak to the power of having a place "where everybody knows your name." The point is, if you want to get serious about influencing the hearts of this generation, you have to think about creating an actual, visible, consistent place where they know they belong.

A few years ago during a message, I (Reggie) was teaching at our annual Orange Conference and I had my daughter Hannah come up with me. She's an amazing artist and the fact that she's graduated from painting on our walls to painting on a professional canvas made her the perfect candidate to help me express this idea. As I began teaching this concept to the room, she began painting, and each word created a new brushstroke. By the end she had painted this beautiful table surrounded by every kind of chair you can think of. Across the canvas was painted the phrase, "There is always a place for you."

That's our role. To provide a place where there's always room at the table for a kid or teenager. To create a space where they know they belong.

From that point on we've used a chair to represent the idea of inclusion. The idea that the church should be the safest place. Where every kid or teenager can find their seat at the table.

When it comes to designing environments, no organization has more opportunity than the church. Unfortunately, some of us have insisted for a long time the Church is not a place, but rather it's people. Maybe we've forgotten that people still need a place. And that, realistically, the Church is both.

For nearly two thousand years, the Church has met in homes, catacombs, restaurants, buildings, cathedrals, tents, theatres, town halls, coffeehouses, storefronts, schools, and hotels. What do all these have in common, besides the fact that they're all nouns? They were actual, physical places where groups of people could meet. Regardless of your denomination or worship style, the local church has always been a place where people can sit down and engage in a learning and worship experience.

The point is, you need a place. Regardless of how you define the Church, you can't ignore that one of its primary functions is to make it easier for people to assemble. The Church has always involved a location. Ideally, the Church may be made up of people, but practically the Church has to assume a responsibility to establish a place where multiple people can actually meet.

Think about it this way:
The Church can't force people to follow Jesus.
The Church can't demand that people embrace the Gospel.
The Church can't dictate that everyone connects relationally.

But the Church *can* create a safe and relevant place for people to engage, learn, and connect. Every church, regardless of its size or budget, can create an environment that makes it easier for kids and teenagers to experience authentic relationships.

It's difficult to lead kids somewhere if you don't know where you're leading them.

One of the most important things your staff should do as a team is prioritize which place is most important in your church. Some churches have so many programs or environments it's easy to have competing systems that confuse people and dilute their potential to influence a kid's faith. That's why we think every church should ask this key question, "Where do you want someone to be?" If we amplified this question, we could say it in a number of ways.

- Where do you want kids to ultimately be so you can influence their faith and character?
- Where is the most optimal environment in your church for kids to have the best potential to grow in their relationship with Jesus Christ?
- If every week, kids or teenagers can only show up one time, experience one environment, participate in one activity, where would you tell them to go?

Every church needs to ask and answer questions like these if they hope to lead kids to a more authentic faith. Since you have limited resources, volunteers, and time, it's essential to prioritize which environment in your church is most important. It's difficult to lead kids somewhere if you don't know where you're leading them. So, what's your answer to the question, "Where do you want kids to be?"

Is it Sunday school?

Is it children's church?

Or is it Activate Live? (The weekly program for your teenagers— not the yogurt.)

Go ahead and decide. Until you do, you can't really be strategic in how you organize your ministry. We think the best answer to the question is:

Whichever environment connects a small group of kids with a consistent leader.

(If we were in a restaurant eating lunch, this is when we'd draw a dot and a circle to represent a small group and a leader.)

Generally speaking, we use these terms to clarify two big ideas:

Small group: a consistent gathering of a few for the purpose of growing in their relationship with God and each other.

Small group leader (SGL): someone who chooses to invest in the lives of a few to encourage authentic faith.

So, if you ask us the question, "Where do you want kids or teenagers to be?" Our answer will be, "in a small group." You can pick a different answer, but just remember: everything else in your culture will be affected by how you respond to this question. When you create a relationally driven culture, you establish a priority with everyone in your ministry that everything you do should somehow point to relationships. We think that if relationships really matter, then small groups should become the primary focus of your ministry strategy.

ACT LIKE YOU BELIEVE IT

What you practice has a direct effect on what you believe. And what you believe has a definite impact what you practice.

Sometimes it's hard to know which one is driving the patterns you see in your organization. But they both have profound influence in your culture.

I (Reggie) remember listening to a lead pastor of a church explain how he had built his church. At one point in the message, he stated, "We don't do small groups at our church. We tried them, and they just didn't work." The speaker who followed him was a friend of mine, and I smiled when he leaned over to me and said, "He's right, I've been to his church and groups don't work at his church." He knew what we all knew. This pastor never modeled or championed groups personally. If you don't act like groups are a priority, then they won't ever be one. **If the leaders in your culture don't really behave like groups are important, then they won't be important.** Simply put, your behavior has a way of determining your belief.

I've been to that same "no-small-groups" church. The children's ministry environments are breathtaking. State-of-the-art technology adorns every entrance. Hallways and rooms are designed with jaw-dropping visuals that highlight the theme for each teaching series. They value excellence in everything they create. It's a church wonderland for any child.

There was only one problem. The ministry wasn't organized so children could interact with the same adult leaders every week. So each time kids showed up, they were ushered to tables with leaders who didn't really know them. Why? The pastor sent a clear message about what should be the priority. The church offered multiple Sunday morning services and the pastor wanted the children's ministry to stay flexible. (That's a pretty good sign that the primary role of children's ministry is to keep the kids busy so parents can go to church.) The pastor didn't want to create the expectation that families should come to the same hour every week. He was concerned if they got up late and missed their hour, they wouldn't come at all. That one decision made it extremely difficult for kids to be connected to the same leader each week and it created a pattern of behavior or a culture where small groups could never really work.

That decision communicated something else too: That what happened on the church's stage was more important than what happened in relationships. The church leaders behaved like drawing a crowd was more important than connecting in a circle. This approach to children's ministry was just one example of how the church devalued small groups.

Maybe that's part of the reason small groups never took off in their church. When small groups aren't a priority everywhere, it's hard for them to be a priority anywhere. People are smarter than you think. No matter what you say you believe, people can tell what's important by the way you act. And your behavior will affect what they believe.

Maybe people decide small groups don't work because their church leaders don't act like they believe small groups really work.

We understand you might be . . .
a "part-time" volunteer
a staff member over the three-year-olds room
an adult service programming director
a craft coordinator
a pizza orderer.

We realize you might not be able to walk up to your church and say, "Hi, I'm reading a book and I have a new strategy that will only work on a church-wide basis, so could you please agree so I can get to work?"

Don't worry. That's not our advice.

Yes, a small group strategy works best when it's the answer for your entire church.

Yes, a small group strategy works when it's the answer for your specific age-group ministry.

In any context of ministry, a relational strategy improves the experience for a kid or teenager. There will be challenges—from your church structure to your church size—but we always say the task is too important not to try something new.

Several years ago, a pastor asked me (Shef) to meet with his elders and staff to help them evaluate their church. They had recently transitioned to a small group model and wanted to discuss ways to improve. After a few hours of talking through their strategy, one of the leaders asked this question: "What do you think is the best discipleship program for our Wednesday night gatherings?" Surprised by his question, I replied, "So you have a discipleship program at your church in the middle of the week as well as Sunday morning small groups?" He said, "Yes, we're just not sure that groups will really be the ultimate answer for discipleship." I responded, "Then they probably never will be the answer."

When he looked confused, I explained, "As long as you have another answer, groups will probably never become *the* answer. If you want small groups to actually become the primary way you disciple people, then you need to start acting like you believe small groups are the best way to disciple people." Our point here isn't that a certain day of the week or timeframe is better than another. Our point is you give energy to what you believe in most. If you say you believe small groups are the answer, but you don't actually act like it, your leaders are smart enough to know the difference.

So, it's simple. If you believe the best way to disciple people is to organize them into small groups, then act like it. When you create multiple options to disciple someone, you risk establishing competing systems that will ensure nothing works well. Again, too many answers can guarantee nobody really knows the answer. As long as you act like something else is really the answer then it probably will be.

> **If small groups become the primary answer, then that ultimately changes everything you do.**

That's why if you believe small groups should be the answer, you should reorganize so they are the answer. Start acting like . . .

1. **Small groups are the answer to everything.**
   How do we disciple kids and teenagers?
   Small groups.
   How do we nurture an ongoing relationship with parents?
   Small groups.
   How do we plug students into service opportunities?
   Small groups.
   How do we evaluate what's working in our ministry?
   Small groups.
   How do we give someone a sense of belonging?
   Small groups.
   How do we monitor what's happening in kids' weekly lives?
   GPS tracking devices maybe, or . . . small groups.

2. **Small group are the answer everywhere.**
   You'll know that you've made small groups the focus when every age-group pastor or ministry leader also has the same answer. When you hear too many different answers, that usually indicates nobody knows the answer. That's why a small group culture tends to put everyone on the same page and creates synergy with the team. Not only should all roads lead to small groups, but all voices should as well. Alignment on a team will make a critical difference in your church. When everyone on your staff is saying the same thing, it will move everyone in your church in the same direction.

If small groups become the primary answer, then that ultimately changes everything you do. Think about it this way: If a strategy is defined as a plan of action with an end in mind, then small groups become the end in mind.

SHIFTING YOUR CULTURE

The rest of this book is about how to create a culture that makes small groups a priority. We think that when relationships matter in your church, you'll tend to value and practice three things.

1. IMPROVE YOUR STRUCTURE
to make relationships matter.

That's because *the quality of your relationships is linked to the quality of your structure.*

It might seem strange to put the words "structure" and "relationships" in the same sentence. They seem like unrelated topics, but we believe they're dependent on each other. Most people need some type of structure to help them connect consistently. Your potential to be successful in connecting people relationally is directly linked to how you organize your ministry. And when you actually start believing people need some type of organization to connect, then you'll be more likely to practice the following behaviors.

This means you'll spend time tweaking the systems in your organization to help people connect effectively. It suggests that someone on your staff—whether paid or volunteer staff—will make leading a group strategy their focus. They'll assume a variety of responsibilities that will include monitoring what is and is not working, arranging and re-arranging how people are organized in groups, and leveraging various platforms to lead people into small groups. The structure includes how you organize your programming and staff. So, what should your structure look like if it's designed to move people toward small groups?

Your PROGRAMMING should lead people to small groups.

- ☐ You'll start evaluating your programs on the basis of whether they complement or compete with groups.
- ☐ You'll tweak programs so they can move people to a small group more effectively, and you'll learn to stop doing things that don't really lead anywhere.
- ☐ You'll shift from creating special events or camps for just kids or teenagers individually to an emphasis on events for small groups to attend together.

Your TEAM should lead people to small groups.

- ☐ You'll reorganize your staff or core volunteer team to make sure someone is focused on making small groups win.
- ☐ You'll hire or recruit organizational leaders who think more strategically about how to arrange groups and track progress.
- ☐ You'll see the advantage of having consistent meetings for various age-group directors or pastors to improve the overall small group structure.

2. EMPOWER LEADERS who make relationships matter.

That's because *the depth of relationships is determined by your investment in leaders.*

Every smart leader should embrace the idea that a ministry to kids or teenagers should never be built around one person. If you don't, you may promote a "pied piper" style of leadership that leads to a very unhealthy culture. It's possible you can become a barrier to discipleship if you decide you should be the one who disciples everyone. We hope that you, as a leader, are self-aware enough to know you have a limited capacity. If you expect to be successful at building a place where kids belong, then your smartest move is to empower leaders—specifically SGLs—to do it.

When every volunteer, leader, and parent champions small groups as a priority, your ministry will develop a different kind of momentum. If you hope to give more kids a genuine sense of belonging, then you'll need more leaders. Don't forget: You can't disciple kids in a crowd. Kids need to be in a context where they're known by someone if you hope to influence their faith. That's why you make recruiting, training, and developing leaders a priority. It's simple. If you want small group leaders to make a weekly investment in kids, then you need to make a weekly investment in small group leaders. How do you know when your leaders are leading? Here are a few ways you can tell.

Your VOLUNTEERS should lead people to small groups.

- ☐ You'll make sure that every volunteer understands specifically how their role helps small groups win.
- ☐ You'll elevate those who volunteer to lead small groups as the most critical in your organization.
- ☐ You'll mobilize teenagers to partner with adults to lead small groups of preschoolers and kids.

Your PARENTS should lead people to small groups.

- ☐ You'll invite parents into a strategic partnership with small groups so they know they have an advocate for their family.
- ☐ You'll help parents connect with small group leaders so they can support each other in helping kids grow spiritually.
- ☐ You'll think about ways to resource both leaders and parents to synchronize them in a comprehensive strategy for kids and teenagers.

3. CREATE EXPERIENCES
where relationships matter.

That's because *the impact of your message is amplified in the context of personal relationships.*

Here's the truth about truth. Kids tend to care more about what you say when they know you care about them. They're not compelled to embrace something simply because it's true. As far as they're concerned, it doesn't matter if it's true. It matters when it matters to them, and it matters even more when they know they matter to you. Does that mean it isn't important to teach or communicate truth? No. It just means you need to recognize that your message is best understood and received in the context of a caring relationship.

This leads us back to the one thing you can most effectively do as a ministry leader: You can create an experience where kids have a better chance to connect with a small group leader. Think about it. You can't make kids believe or force them to have deeper relationships. But you can create a place that makes it easier for them to belong and believe. That's why you have to work diligently to shape the weekly experience that's actually happening for the average kid.

Your ENVIRONMENTS lead people to small groups.
- ☐ You'll leverage every platform to promote and explain how to connect in small groups.
- ☐ You'll draw a clearer distinction between those who teach and those who lead kids.
- ☐ You'll spotlight small group leaders to raise the value of their role within the environment.

Your CURRICULUM should lead people to small groups.
- ☐ You'll craft large group presentations so they enhance the activity and connection within the small group.
- ☐ You'll give priority focus to creating effective small group activities and discussion.
- ☐ You'll guard the amount of time allotted for small group activity.

When relationships matter, you tend to move things around in your organization so everything points to small groups. It's interesting how simply re-arranging the furniture in a room can enhance or inhibit how people relate and connect. But that's one of your main jobs as a next generation leader. Hopefully, these next chapters will help you sharpen your skills. If you want to create a culture where small groups flourish, then you need to have an ongoing plan for what happens with your structure, leaders, and experiences. If you're interested in having such a plan, then keep reading. That's what the rest of this book is about.

IMPROVE YOUR STRUCTURE
SO RELATIONSHIPS MATTER.

That's because the quality of your relationships is linked to the quality of your structure.

Relationships don't just happen without . . .

an introduction.

an invitation.

a calendar.

a place to sit down.

some type of initiative on someone's part.

The point is: It takes a number of things working behind the scenes for relationships to happen. These things don't guarantee strong relationships, but they facilitate the possibility of people connecting. Before most relationships happen . . .

Someone has to make the first move.
Someone has to set a time.
Someone has to start the conversation.
Someone has to find a place to meet.

Relationships don't just happen.
They require some degree of initiative and intentionality.

Do you know why some small groups work and others don't?
We're going to make a suggestion that may seem counterintuitive.

Relationships need structure.

Now, before alarms go off in your head and you imagine a rigid routine to build better friendships, let's clarify. Like we said, it seems strange to put the words *relationships* and *structure* in the same sentence. But a healthy amount of structure can fuel people so they can grow relationally.

Here's how we define structure:
"How you arrange or manage various parts so they can support something important."

If we translate that for you as a ministry leader, we could ask the question this way:

"How do you arrange or manage staff, volunteers, programs, budget, calendar, or even those who attend each week so everything supports a relational model?"

Structure matters more than most leaders realize.

The right kind of structure can help things grow. Think about it.

What if a farmer only planted seeds randomly?
What if athletes only exercised when they felt like it?
What if a CEO rarely looked at the budget?
What if a pastor never prepared his sermon?

Okay, I know it might seem like that last one happens a lot.
But the point is, without some intentional structure . . .
things don't grow the right way,
things usually don't move in a positive direction,
and things can't really improve.

Why are we quick to agree that structure helps most things grow,
but somehow forget how much it matters in relationships?

Let's think about this. We realize we need structure for our faith to
grow. Isn't that why . . .
God commanded us to take a day each week to recharge our faith?
Moses said to talk to your kids about their faith every morning
and night?
Jesus suggested that we pray daily?
Your church probably plans a series on spiritual disciplines
every year?

So, consider the question another way:
*If structure can help you grow your business, your health, and
your faith, why doesn't structure matter when you're trying to help
people grow relationally?*

If you really believe the quality of your relationships is linked to the quality of your structure, then you should try to improve your structure so relationships can thrive.

Have you ever considered that whatever tends to work in your church is working because you've improved your present structure to support it? You provide support for what you think is important.

Chances are . . .
You have a structure to support your Sunday morning services.
You have a structure to support global and local mission efforts.
You have a structure to support various education and ministry programs.
You even have a structure to support every kid who needs to poop.
But what kind of structure do you have to support the kind of relationships that will help people grow?

Your church should have systems in place to help people grow in their relationship with God and each other. You should be intentional about connecting people to people.

We read a blog by a pastor who had been critical of small groups. He believed that groups don't work for people, and that most people don't naturally grow in a group context. He argued that the significant relationships that had affected his spiritual formation just happened naturally. He even said small groups were a westernized concept that had adversely affected the potential of people to experience authentic and Biblical community.

The more we read, the clearer it became that his response seemed to be a reaction to unhealthy small group models. He was disillusioned with a version of small groups that was unfocused, poorly led, and characterized by fill-in-the blank Bible studies. (It was also apparent that many of his descriptions referred to adult groups.) Still, we respected this leader and share some of the same concerns when small groups aren't structured well. Interestingly, after a few years, he came back around as a believer in the idea that the right small group strategy can be a springboard for discipleship.

That being said, there are few things I'd like to state as disclaimers about building a structure that supports small groups.

No small group model is perfect.
(unless you recruit perfect leaders and create a flawless organization)

All small groups are not created equal.
(unless you're better at matching people than ChristianMingle.com)

Some people will need to go even smaller than small groups.
(unless nobody in your group ever needs counseling or mentoring)

Small groups will need to be constantly tweaked.
(unless you discover the secret formula that works for everyone, forever)

I hope there will always be smart critics around to challenge us to the best answers. (Of course, the world would be a lot better with fewer *mean* critics.) Our mission is too important to not ask hard questions so we can evaluate and improve what we do.

Sometimes, those who are hyper-critical about small groups are frustrated by a system where the structure is either almost non-existent or far too rigid.

But when a team works to build and refine the right culture, we believe the most efficient way to connect kids and teenagers relationally is a healthy small group supported by the right kind of structure. In its best expressions, a small group paves the way for kids and teens to build a strong relationships with a leader who can personally disciple them. At a minimum, it gives them a place to belong and introduces them to a consistent leader to nudge them in a positive direction in their faith.

If you want small groups to work in your ministry, you need to believe and behave like relationships don't just happen. Even if you can point to scenarios where relationships appeared to happen by chance, I suspect someone was still being intentional, something was still being arranged, and there was still a degree of structure. Sure, sometimes there can be a kind of a relational magic that appears like a campfire on a perfect starry night. But it's rare, and not everyone will experience it.

For the rest of the world, where many people are not as extroverted,
or driven,
or committed,
or persuaded,
or believers,
or leaders,
we needs to have an alternative plan to encourage relational connections.

Happy relational accidents might sometimes happen, but most people still need a structure that makes it easier for them to find a place that's welcoming, safe, and sacred.

Be careful that you don't promote a version of church that's just for the few and the committed.

Churches should aggressively confront the notion that discipleship is reserved for a certain kind of Christians who think exactly alike. If we don't challenge that mindset, those outside the walls of the church will never venture inside. Just remember: We aren't called to disciple Christians who are trying to build community with other Christians. We're called to simply "make disciples." The early disciples didn't go into the world to find people who already believed so they could help them believe more deeply. They went on a rescue mission to find people who weren't following Jesus so they could lead them to start following Jesus.

We think, as it relates to kids and teenagers, it's even more important to influence the structure they need to build relationships.

Unless you assume kids will just figure out how to connect on their own . . .
Unless you believe that relationships don't need a prompt or a cue . . .
Unless you buy into the notion teenagers naturally move toward positive friendships . . .
Unless you simply believe you don't need a plan to help relationships grow . . .
You need to do something intentional.

Your church is surrounded by kids and teenagers who are guarded, isolated, skeptical, and vulnerable. If you're going to give them a place to belong, it will require extra effort on your part as leader.

It's simple.

If you believe someone's faith is best developed through authentic community, then you should improve your structure so it supports relationships. Most leaders understand relationships need a nudge or a prod, and are trying to do something about it. We suggest that if you don't know exactly what to do, then start designing a structure that supports small groups.

Unless, of course, you think community just happens by accident—then your job is easy. Just sit back and wait for it to happen by itself. Let's see how well that works.

ORGANIZE TO BE MORE ORGANIC
(Let's talk about your staff.)

---

opefully you're not content to sit back and let relationships just happen.
So, why don't you start improving your structure?

Get ready to do a little organizing and arranging.
Get ready to set a few rules.

Here's an idea. Go find the singularly most organized and inflexible person you know, and hire them to manage your small groups. Put them in charge of optimizing how your small groups will be arranged for everyone, forever. Make sure your kindergartners understand the sacredness of their groups—preferably by having them sign a covenant committing to stay in their designated group for a pre-determined amount of time. After all, you want to make sure you give kids some stability.

Or, if that sounds too rigid, maybe you want to try something a little different. Even though we believe structure is essential for relationships, we probably all agree that too much structure can shut some relationships down.

Some people want to schedule their own calendar.
Some people don't want to be forced to share private thoughts.
Some people even like to have a say in who their friends are.

When I (Kristen) was 12, I asked to bring a friend on our family vacation. Traditionally, my family went to the beach with another family who had a little girl about the age of my younger sister. But that year I was more interested in listening to Tracy Bird sing "Keeper of the Stars" while I got just-enough-burned on the beach than watching *Homeward Bound* and boogie-boarding with the jellyfish. My mom's friend wasn't comfortable with me bringing a stranger, so she came up with a better plan. They'd choose a friend for me. They knew someone my age who would be "just perfect."

If you've ever . . .
been set up on a date,
been randomly assigned college roommates,
or had your mom's friend choose your beach buddy,
then you probably know it's difficult to force relationships.

We've all been there. We know what it's like to try to manufacture a connection that feels disingenuous, artificial, or forced.

But there's a fine line between too much structure and not quite enough. A relationally driven model has to be supported with the right amount of structure. So, how do you know if you have enough structure? How do you know if you have too much?

There's not a magic formula. There's no set of rules to determine how much structure you need. And we know this: Your team will probably not agree about it. (This may come as a shock, since I'm sure you agree about everything else.) People are wired differently. Evidently, God has a sense of humor, because He created a wide variety of people who have different outlooks when it comes to the amount of structure and order they prefer.

Some people plan vacations down to the minute,
while others prefer to decide each day as it comes.

Some people have a family calendar in a prominent place in their home, while others haven't written a date on the calendar in their entire lives.

In this crazy world of differing opinions about how much structure is helpful for relationships to thrive, let's agree on this:

Relationships need structure, but structure isn't the goal. The goal is relational connection.

> **""**
>
> # Relationships need structure, but structure isn't the goal. The goal is relational connection.

The goal is for a kid to feel known by someone, and to feel like they belong somewhere. If that's happening, chances are you've created the right amount of structure.

Still not clear? Maybe we can say it this way:

You may need to create a little more structure for your groups if . . .
Kids can't name one other person in their small group.
You aren't sure when or where groups are meeting.
SGLs are unclear about the purpose of a group.

You may have let structure get out of control when . . .
You've never allowed a kid to switch groups.
You dictate exactly when and where everyone meets.
SGLs are afraid of trying something new or deviating from your script.

When you organize to be organic, you create a structure that supports what's most important. You're inclined to implement a system of guiding principles rather than absolute rules. You delegate freely to SGLs who will adapt and change what needs to be changed in order to achieve the desired result. Which brings us to one of the first things you should consider when it comes to structure.

When you organize to be organic . . .
SOMEONE HAS TO OWN IT.

If groups are a priority in your ministry, someone needs to feel responsible for groups. You've probably already thought of that, but we wanted to make it really clear. It's actually why we wrote this book. You might consider the three values and nine practices in this book as the job description for whoever is in charge of small groups.

First, you have to decide who will own it.

Maybe you own it—along with a whole bunch of other things.
Maybe you share these responsibilities with another staff member.
Maybe you hire someone specifically for this role.
Maybe you have a highly committed volunteer who owns it.

It's up to you to decide who owns it. But just remember, without focused, designated attention, groups will never work the way they should. In some ways, *small* actually takes more structure than *large*.

Nina Schmidgall leads the family ministry team at National Community Church in Washington, D.C. As a multi-site church, they started with a handful of small locations in movie theaters connected to train stations. When she talked about what led them to a "lead small" approach," Nina said, "The thing that convinced us to be a lead small culture was growth. When we started, each of our locations had such a small number of kids that every campus *was* a small group. As our locations grew, we realized we were missing something. We wanted to put the emphasis back on relationships, and we knew we needed to structure things to get back there."

Something remarkable happened in Nina's ministry when it was small—because it was small. Relationships were helping kids grow an authentic faith. Then as they grew larger, they had to get *more* intentional about structuring their ministry so they could keep relational connections strong.

TWO SIDES OF A MINISTRY

Regardless of your church size, there are probably two components to your weekly ministry:
- **PROGRAMMING — what happens on the platform, or at the front of the room while people watch.**
- **GROUPS — what happens in circles, or coffee houses, or bowling alleys while kids and teenagers participate.**

When it comes to your staff, your hiring ratios for these two components aren't the same.

If you're just starting out or you're in a smaller church, maybe your hiring ratios are simple. It's just you. But you can apply this next principle to the percentage of attention, focus, or volunteers you designate to each component.

Quality production takes talented people. But it takes roughly the same number of people to produce an event whether you have 50 or 500 in attendance. The same thing isn't true for groups. Just like you need more SGLs for 400 kids than you would for 20, you can't support 30 SGLs with the same number of staff that it took for only five. Your ratios are different. We'll talk more specifically in the next section about the kind of attention your SGLs need. But for now let's just say: before you can even begin to give your groups the structure they need, someone has to own it.

When you organize to be organic . . .
AGE CHANGES THE RULES.

Remember the story about getting set up with a friend for the beach? That story may not make a lot of sense to someone who spends time working with toddlers and younger elementary kids. Why? Well, the postman could probably pick a playmate for a toddler with relative success. It might not be a friendship that takes off, but you stand a pretty good chance of making it work.

If you work with older elementary, tweens, or teenagers, things are different. They have stronger opinions about who they hang out with and how they spend their time. Things change, and they want more independence and control over their world.

Here's a basic principle when it comes to improving the structure for kids:
The younger they are, the more structure they need.

Small groups for two- and three-year-olds don't look the same as small groups for middle-schoolers. They're at very different stages, so the way you structure the groups should be different.

You might want to look at it this way . . .

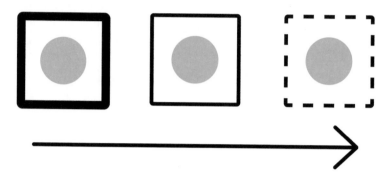

When you oversee groups for younger kids, you need to exercise a higher level of control over things like time, place, snacks, and activities. As kids get older, your structure should provide enough flexibility for kids to determine how the group works best for them.

When I (Kristen) was leading a group of high school juniors several years ago, I remember watching another SGL do something I thought was remarkable. This particular leader had a group of seniors who had been together for four years. When the time came for our annual February retreat, her seniors were "so over it."

They'd been doing retreats like these since sixth grade, and there was a "been there, done that" mentality. Instead of launching into a campaign of shame to make sure her seniors knew their spiritual maturity was dependent on their attendance at this event, this leader went a different direction. She sought counsel from our church leadership, and they jointly decided to create a second option for her group. Her group spent the weekend of the retreat on a small group retreat of their own. The church gave that leader the same material they'd be covering at the event, and the leader customized it for her seniors. They were able to cover the same topic, but on a level that was specific for them as almost-graduates.

What kind of impact do you think that weekend made on her group of seniors?

The older they are, the more flexible your structure should be.

Now, before you disagree and start writing a blog post about how student ministries need their seniors to be fully engaged so they can lead their peers, hold on. That's true. Juniors and seniors shouldn't be encouraged to check out of student ministry. When you improve your structure in the right way, there will be seniors who are committed not only to attending, but to plugging in to serve and lead in student ministry. But that won't be every senior. Some will be ready to move beyond what they've been doing for the past several years. So, if you lead a student ministry you should ask yourself this question: Does our structure have enough flexibility to maintain influence with those who are ready for something different?

If your only discipleship option for students (especially seniors) is for them to keep attending what they no longer want to attend, then maybe you should rethink your structure. You can't force students to come at a specific time or to a specific place any more than you can choose their best friend. You may need to become a little more organic.

When you organize to be more organic . . .
EVERYONE NEEDS A GOOD SEAT.

Your staff may never find a formula that ensures every kid will connect with their SGL and their group. But someone on your staff (the one who owns small groups) will constantly be placing kids in a group. They'll be looking for ways to give kids a better group experience. They'll do their best to give every kid a better seat.

A better seat will give a kid a better chance to . . .
see God.
connect with other believers.
grow in their faith.
meet their soul-mate.

Okay, maybe not that last one. But we do think where and how you place kids in groups has the potential to support group connection. Here are three priorities we think can help you give kids a better seat.

1. FEWER IS BETTER

So, what are optimal small group ratios? We don't really know. But we asked dozens of smart leaders who have created and sustained a healthy small group culture in their ministries, and here are the averages they gave us:

Preschool: 5-7

Elementary: 8-12

Middle School and High School: 8-12

Not every leader has the same relational capacity. Not every small group has the same level of consistency. Not every kid requires the same level of attention. For those reasons, you may never have a one-size-fits-all ratio for groups. But whenever you think about optimal group ratios, remember this: Fewer is better. Then make adjustments based on a few other considerations.

When you think about your group ratios, consider the attendance patterns of your audience. For example, Kevin Ragsdale, who has been leading ministry teams for North Point Ministries for over 15 years, likes to place no more than 12 on a small group roll, so there will be an average of eight who show up weekly. As you make group placements, think about how often you expect kids to show up.

When you think about your group ratios, consider the typical growth of a group. You can also intentionally start groups smaller so they have room to grow throughout the year.

When you think about your group ratios, consider what you're asking leaders to do. If you encourage leaders to connect with every kid on their roster, regardless of whether or not they show up in the room, there will ultimately be a limit to how many kids you can assign to an SGL.

2.COMMON INTERESTS MATTER

In the months leading up to your Promotion Sunday, the person in your ministry who owns small groups will have the task of placing kids in a group. That's a lot of responsibility. So, how will your ministry decide which kids go where?

After talking with leaders who have spent years placing kids in groups, the general consensus looks something like this:

GENDER > AGE > ADDRESS > PREFERENCES

If we had to unpack that a little more, we would say two things determine the way you will approach group placement.

The size of your ministry

If you have a ministry of eight kids, it's simple. They all go in one group. But once your numbers start to grow, things get complicated. The larger your ministry, the more intentionality you'll have to give to this question. The larger your ministry, the more layers you'll need to add in order to place kids in groups.

The age of the kids

The system you create for placing preschoolers will probably look different than the system you use for placing high schoolers. For example, if you work with younger kids, gender may not be a factor when placing kids in group. Most leaders say they have mixed-gender small groups for kids until around third grade. Then they begin to separate guy groups from girl groups.

Remember, the older the kid, the more flexible the structure needs to be. That means staff who oversee older age-groups will need more ways to filter groups so kids can connect.

When Kevin Ragsdale started InsideOut, the student ministry at North Point, it included middle and high school age groups together. His goal was always to one day split the ministry into age-specific programs. He also knew he wanted their small groups to be divided by gender, grade, school, or geographic location, and friends, interests, hobbies, etc. That was the dream. However, when they started, there were only around 40 students sixth through twelfth grade showing up on a consistent basis. Kevin said, "This caused us to look at our group structure in a completely different way. We followed the same guidelines, but we also adjusted groups based on the number of students in each specific grade. In some cases, we put multiple grades together. We have always divided middle and high school students by gender regardless of the numbers. But early on we had sixth, seventh, eighth, and ninth grade guys together in one group, one tenth-grade guys group, and one eleventh-and-twelfth-grade guys group. The same thing happened with our girls groups." Again, this was based on how many students were showing up from a specific grade. As more students started attending, they began to divide the grades and then subdivide based on location and interests because he knew, ultimately, the end goal for his group structure.

3.GUESTS ARE ALWAYS WELCOME

The good news is, once you place every kid into a group, your job is done until next year. No one will move away. No one will come for the first time. Everyone will be happy with the group you selected for them, and you'll never have to make an adjustment—unless of course you're working with real people instead of playing The Sims.

That's why there's an organic nature to group placement.

It's also why we don't think closed groups for kids and teenagers are a good idea.

Sometimes we hear leaders advocate for a small group system where guests aren't welcome. Their arguments seem to be based on the idea that in order for kids to go "deeper" with their discipleship, they need to be surrounded by kids who are "as seasoned" in their faith. We think there's a false dichotomy between going deeper and being evangelistically driven. Sometimes including new kids in a group is exactly what that group needs in order to help kids move toward a more authentic faith.

When you give kids a closed group, you . . .
set them up to believe faith is only for insiders.
rob them of an opportunity to share their faith with others.
limit the questions that will be processed in the group context.

If guests are always welcome, you plan for them to show up. You create a system for assimilating them into a group as smoothly as possible. Your system should be customized according to your church size and the age group of your kids. But if you're looking for ideas, here are a few specific ways other leaders handle assimilation:

At National Community Church, Nina Schmidgall combined new kids according to their age, "When new kids visit one of the NCC campuses, they simply join their age group. If we just put all new or visiting kids together, they would be with kids of drastically different ages."

Amy Fenton, who served as a Children's Ministry Director in Franklin, Tennessee, shared that at The People's Church they included their greeters in the process. "When we have a guest, I always ask the greeters to let kids see if they know someone first. If they do, we let them visit that group. We know that seeing a familiar face will make them more comfortable."

At North Point, Kevin Ragsdale developed "on-deck" groups. "When a student comes to InsideOut for the first time, they go to an 'on-deck' group," Kevin explained. "In 'on-deck' students are invited to meet the staff, and hear an overview of our ministry. Then they fill out a survey to give us some information about their interests. If they come back a second time, we have placed them in a group and given their new leader their survey."

Jenny Zimmer has been leading as Family Life Director at California's Discovery Church, specifically in the preschool environment. She said, "We have a 'special small group' for first-time visitors. They go into this small group until the parent decides what service is a best fit for them."

No matter what system you create to assimilate new kids into small groups, you need some structure around it. You need someone on your staff to own it. And you may have to do some arranging and re-arranging if you want to give groups the right amount of structure so they can thrive. That's why you organize to be organic.

When you get in the habit of organizing to be organic, what everyone does works together to make relationships matter.

THINK STEPS, NOT PROGRAMS
(Let's talk about your programs.)

When I (Reggie) first started working as a student pastor, I thought my goal was to create as many effective programs as possible.

It seemed logical.

More programs meant more opportunities to keep teenagers out of trouble.
More programs meant more options to reach a variety of students.
More programs meant more volunteers investing in teenagers.
More programs meant more students learning truth.

Oh, and if I'm really honest,
more programs meant I looked more successful as a leader.

I had a host of programs that were somewhat successful. That is, if you measure success by how many participate, or the number of compliments you get from leaders or parents. But I wish someone had explained to me in my first decade of ministry what I learned in the last two decades.

It's important to clarify the primary win in your ministry before you can evaluate if a specific program is successful.

When you think about the programs in your ministry, here's a strategic question to ask.
"Did the program help you move people in the direction you want them to go?"

Of course that implies you know where you want them to go. Remember, we think the win for your ministry is connecting kids in a healthy small group. If you agree, then evaluate the programs in your ministry to see if they're helping or hindering small groups.

Here's a sobering possibility.
Some programs in your ministry may be working so well they're keeping something more important from working.

As long as you have limited facilities, volunteers, budget, calendar, and energy, you have to prioritize those resources around what you think is most important. So if you want small groups to win, you need to take a hard look at the rest of what you do.

One of three things will be true about your programs.
They're moving kids away from small groups.
They're moving kids toward small groups.
They're not moving kids anywhere.

In the early days of North Point Community Church, a few leaders approached us about implementing a program for new moms. It seemed like an easy win. These were seasoned and responsible leaders (who promised they would do all of the work). They had enormous influence and passion for this ministry. They also had the resources of a reputable national organization behind the program they wanted to start. And since the program was designed to build a bridge to families who were outside the church, it was easy for us to say yes. Within a few years, the program was extremely successful.

Then, during one of our annual retreats with our ministry directors, I asked a simple question. "Are there any programs we do that aren't helping us move people where we want them to go?" My heart sank when one of our directors named this program, because I knew the battle we'd fight with key leaders if we discontinued it. But we immediately knew she was right. This program had become so popular it had tapped more and more of our best volunteers. It consistently demanded extra facilities, technical support, and budget with every passing season. Our staff had become inundated with problem-solving and managing numerous details for this program. But all of that was secondary to the realization that this program was not strategic in moving people toward groups or deeper relationships. So, we made the hard decision to discontinue.

> **Some programs in your ministry may be working so well they're keeping something more important from working.**

Of course, when we explained our reasoning to the program leaders, they kindly agreed it was the right decision.

That is, after numerous phone calls to the elders and executive staff, a heated petition, and a passionate conversation with the national organization's president. It was a painful and agonizing process. But our team was confident it was the right thing to do, because the program had become a competing system that was hindering what we wanted to happen relationally with families.

Just remember this:
Sometimes you have to stop doing something that works if you want something more important to work better.

From time to time you have to re-evaluate everything you do if you want to gain new momentum in the critical areas of your ministry. One of the keys to building an effective ministry is distinguishing between random programs and strategic programs.

Random programs are created to meet various needs.
Strategic programs are created to lead people to what's next.

Random programs work independently.
Strategic programs work together.

Random programs tend to establish competing systems.
Strategic programs establish complementary systems.

Random programs function as activities.
Strategic programs function as steps.

In *The 7 Practices of Effective Ministry*, Andy Stanley, Lane Jones, and I (Reggie) introduce the practice of "Think Steps, Not Programs." In the book, we explain the importance of evaluating programs to see if they're working as steps to move people relationally in the right direction. We say a program that's working like a step should be easy, clear, and strategic.

Programs should make it *easy*,
not hard, for people to participate and move to what's next.

Programs should be promoted in a *clear* way
so people can actually see how and why they're important.

Programs should be *strategic* in the way
they support the primary goal or priority of the ministry.

As you create a small group culture for kids and teenagers, it's important to rethink the various programs in your ministry so they can function as steps to the small group experience.

When you think steps, not programs . . .
PLATFORMS ENHANCE SMALL GROUPS.

Every program has a platform that can be leveraged to influence people to value groups. If you want parents, kids, and teenagers to believe small group is important, then what you say about small groups on every platform is important.

CASTING VISION
We're sure most people are such fans of what you do that they heard your vision once and are now raving fans forever. But the rest of the crowd is going to leave your church this week and do their normal routine of wakeboarding, cave spelunking, or watching the latest Marvel superheroes movie. In their case, you

may need to look for creative ways to keep them thinking about the value of small groups. Just remember: It's the nature of a vision to leak. So they may need to hear it again, and again, and again in as many creative ways as possible if you want them to make groups a consistent priority.

The value of small groups can be communicated by . . .
a story in the pastor's sermon.
a video before a program starts.
a clever, funny announcement.
an interview with a small group leader.

All of these things can help parents understand your strategy a little better, too. They can explain why parents should commit to attending the same hour every week, or why kids are getting a random postcard in the mail from another adult, or why their second-grade daughter dressed in pajamas to go to church.

Part of the success of every program should be linked to how well it elevates the idea of finding authentic community. Program directors should consider asking and answering the question, "What can we say or do to help people know what's next?" Whenever there's reluctance or resistance to championing small groups from a platform, it may be an indicator that a program is out of sync or no longer strategic.

MANAGING TIME

Nothing communicates the value of the small group or a small group leader any more than how you structure time. If a speaker goes for forty minutes and small group lasts for ten, it suggests what's happening on the platform is at least four times more important than what's happening in small group. (It may also suggest someone doesn't understand the attention span of a four-year-old boy.)

By the way, cheating your small group leaders out of time with their group is also a great way to get rid of your best SGLs. Smart leaders can tell what matters most by how you arrange the segments in your program. Our surveys indicate an average small group should get about 30 minutes of interaction each week in your programming. Their time together may happen at multiple points in the overall experience. For example, in the elementary ages you may open with a ten-minute small group activity at the beginning of the hour, and end with fifteen to twenty minutes of more focused small group time later. Your goal is to create a structure that guards the small group time, so it becomes the priority within the program.

At North Point, Kevin Ragsdale said they try to give about 30 minutes for the average small group. "It's also why we do our student groups on Sunday night. That way there's really no time limit on the back end if they're having great discussion. They can even carry the conversation into dinner."

When you think steps, not programs . . .
EVENTS SOLIDIFY SMALL GROUPS.

Those of us who have worked in student ministry are convinced of this one irrefutable fact:
Long bus rides lead to stronger small groups.

Okay, so there's no statistical information to back this up.
But, we think an eight-hour bus ride to a student camp gives a small group leader more credibility in a student's life than at least twenty Sundays. If the bus happens to break down, it probably equals another three months of Sundays in bonding.

Maybe that's why many churches who are building a relationally driven culture rethink how they design and position events (or bus rides) to make small groups win.

Everything event I (Shef) did centered around our small groups. All of our events were groups-based or we didn't do them. Groups, not individuals, were assigned to cabins, buses, and lunchtimes,. We planned our talks for camp by figuring out what we wanted to happen in groups first. The program then became set-up for group. We asked leaders to come with their kids to camp, not help us run camp. The plan was for them to have experiences together as much as possible.

Our friend Darren Kizer, who worked at Parker Hill in Scranton, Pennsylvania, explained to us how he prepped for events. "Our trips and experiences were built with small groups in mind. For example, it was more important to ask, 'How many small groups will be on this trip?' than it was to ask, 'How many students are coming?' I would rather have empty beds in cabins if we had to. Prioritizing for small groups is more important than renting one less room."

RETHINKING CAMPS

I (Reggie) have worked as a speaker and leader at camps for over 30 years. Most of my summers have been spent training student pastors and small group leaders. After years of wrestling with what makes a camp experience work, I've become more determined than ever to help leaders rethink how they do camps. The optimal camp experience happens when the leaders who produce the camp and the churches who bring students both have a shared value related to small groups. Too many camps function more like random events than strategic experiences. Every camp should be designed to have lasting value for the church beyond the week of camp.

A few years ago, I sat down with a host of student pastors to analyze the camp experience. We dreamed about what student camps built around the value of small groups would look like. We came up with ten characteristics that make a student camp small-group friendly.

- Small group leaders, not random adult chaperones, attend with students.
- Main sessions are limited in production and time to complement group.
- Resources are provided during camp to enhance the small group experience.
- SGLs are valued and trained during the camp experience.
- Each camp is built around an age-group focus for relevance.
- Speakers are coached so messages set up small group time.
- Activities or mission opportunities are organized around small groups.
- Churches are provided with a follow-up curriculum for small groups after camp.
- A targeted social media strategy is designed to engage parents with camp.
- Logistics are organized so small group leaders can stay focused on relationships.

Too many camps focus their energy on creating a "wow factor" for the main stage sessions while neglecting to make small groups a priority. Both can happen, but unless the camp leadership authentically values small groups, the production will be the priority. There's a trend at many camps to over-produce and wear kids out physically and emotionally so there's not a lot of energy left to connect in the context of a group.

Those who create camp experiences should take a fresh approach. They should act like what happens in the small group is more important than what happens on the stage.

Think about it this way.
Camp typically lasts a week.
Speakers and worship leaders leave.
Students go back to their church with their small group leaders.
Which relationships do you think are most important?

MAKING EVENTS STRATEGIC
The same logic we apply to camp should be applied to every event. When you create a small group culture, you tend to look at every event through a new lens. You realize events have incredible potential to solidify the relationships in groups.

Now, you may be asking, "What about kids who are visiting, new, or are not yet in a small group?"

A strategic event can actually be one of the best ways to help new kids get connected deeper and faster. Instead of hanging out with a random chaperone who they may never see again, a small-group-focused event will connect kids with SGLs and peers they'll see again if they show up to your weekly experience.

SERVING TOGETHER AS GROUPS
If you've ever taken a group on a mission trip or service project, you know the value these experiences have when it comes to deepening relationships. Time spent taking care of the homeless, working with disadvantaged kids, or becoming actively involved helping a different people group creates a unique sense of teamwork and mission. It's also a great training ground for SGLs and their few to develop ministry skills. When small groups serve together, they can discover something they may not experience through Bible study, prayer, and worship.

When you think steps, not programs . . .
VOLUNTEERS REINFORCE SMALL GROUPS.

Making small groups win is a team sport. Just like your staff structure should support small groups, all other volunteer teams exist to support groups. Let's make a list of some of the non-SGL volunteers you might have for your weekly experience:
Hallway greeters
Room greeters
Large group hosts
Large group presenters/speakers
Production and tech teams
Actors for dramas
Crowd control
Band and worship teams
Food teams
Security
Registration teams
The guy you test your games on

You have a variety of volunteers who have very different jobs. It's easy for everyone to be so hyper-focused on what they do that they miss the bigger picture. That's why it's important to clarify the primary win. When the primary win is defined in terms of an effective small group experience, it will synchronize your volunteer teams so they can work together. When everyone on the team clearly understands the goal, it changes how they do what they do. Let's use a typical high school program to illustrate this principle.

Say you define the primary win for your student ministry as follows:

"We win when a student has meaningful interaction during small group that influences his faith in Jesus and deepens his relationships with others."

Now, imagine if you wrote that win on a board and invited all of your volunteers into the room. After a short explanation of why it's important to give kids a place to belong, you explain the win to everyone. You say something like:

"If you're a HOST on stage, we need you to use transitional statements and champion small group from the platform. Your win happens when you inspire and motivate students to make their small group meaningful."

"If you're a WORSHIP LEADER, we need you to create an environment that breaks down walls and prepares students to be open to hear the message. Your win happens when students are moved to participate together in collective worship."

"If you're the SPEAKER, we need you to position the message to set up small group. Your win happens when what you say becomes a springboard for dynamic and meaningful conversation during small group."

"If you're COOKING hamburgers, we need you to know you're not just cooking hamburgers—you're providing an informal time for groups to connect. Your win happens when students hang around longer after group and go a little deeper in their relationships."

If the message, music, and food are incredible, but kids don't connect in small group, the program wasn't a step.

When you think steps, not programs . . .
RESOURCES SUPPORT SMALL GROUPS.

If you're going to act like you believe small groups are important, then you may need to spend your budget like you believe it. There are a number of resource indicators that small groups are really a priority in your church:

How you build and design your facilities.
How you pay the staff who directs small group ministry.
How you invest to develop SGLs.
How you allocate your budget to help small group activities.

REALLOCATING BUDGET

I (Shef) remember when it first occurred to me that if small groups were our ultimate someplace, we needed to spend our money like we believed it. So I proposed to my team that we slash the programming budget to support small group leaders.

The most impactful decision we made was when we decided to commit to recruiting two small group leaders for each group. At the time we didn't even have one for each group. But in order for our students to have a consistently excellent experience, we were convinced—and still are—that we needed two SGLs.

This decision really hit our budget when it came to camps. We committed early on to never charge a small group leader to go to camp. We wanted to make sure we were communicating to SGLs how much we valued them and the time they sacrificed to be there. Now, instead of paying for just one leader per group, we were paying for two.

We knew this would seem like a big deal to the executive team when it came to our budget. And while that sounds expensive, the reality is, if you divide that cost across 12 to 15 kids in the group, it's a really minimal cost with maximal impact. Sure, this decision automatically doubled our SGL development budget overnight, but it's the best money we ever spent.

It forced us to get creative when it came to other aspects of our programming, like sets, speakers, and content. But at the end of the day, we were finally adding value according to our greatest value.

EVALUATING PROGRAMS

So let's recap.
The programs in your church should function as steps. But chances are . . .

Some programs are not moving people where they need to go.
Some programs are just repeating what you're doing somewhere else.
Some programs are creating competing systems.
Some programs require too much energy for what they actually accomplish.

Why don't you make a list of all the programs in your ministry?

- Circle the programs you can change to be more strategic.
- (Make a specific list of improvements to make them work better.)
- Put an "x" by the programs you should consider killing.
- (Maybe write down a date when you want to bury them. It could make you feel better.)
- Underline the programs that are most strategic.
- Make an additional list of any programs you think you should add.

In all of these cases, you either need to stop something or change something; you can't afford to leave things the way they are.

Several years ago, I (Reggie) was eating dinner with a marketing executive from Nike. He informed me that Steve Jobs had just visited their headquarters and made an intriguing remark that had them rethinking everything.

Jobs had said, "You guys make some incredible products. But you also make a lot of crap. Why don't you just stop making the crap?"

I'm sure your church does some amazing things. But maybe you have some programs that aren't so amazing or strategic. Why don't you stop doing what's less strategic, and do more of what really works? Create programs that work as steps toward relationships.

When you get in the habit of thinking steps, not programs, kids are more likely to end up where you want them to be.

MOVE TO THE RHYTHM
(Let's talk about your calendar.)

Life has a rhythm.

Your life has a rhythm.

You probably brush your teeth before going to bed.
Maybe you get up around the same hour every morning.
You might even shop at the same grocery store when you need
some Double Stuf Oreos.

There's something about having a rhythm to your life that makes
it more comfortable and efficient. Some things move almost
automatically, below the surface, unnoticed. But if you think about
it, there's something about the rhythms of your life that reflect
what you value.
If you brush your teeth, you probably value hygiene.
If you wake up in the morning, maybe it's because you value work.
If you shop for Double Stuf Oreos, well, we're not sure what that
reveals. But you get the point.

What you do in the everyday patterns of life demonstrates what
you value.
And when you do something repeatedly, it can actually make you
value it more.

Maybe that's why when Moses stood on the edge of Canaan and
spoke to the nation of Israel about passing on faith to future
generations, he said this:

These commandments that I give you today are to be on your hearts. Impress them on your children. Talk about them when you sit at home and when you walk along the road, when you lie down and when you get up. Tie them as symbols on your hands and bind them on your foreheads. Write them on the doorframes of your houses and on your gates.[4]

Moses was doing something rather brilliant. He was anchoring the faith of the Israelite people to the natural rhythms of life. If we were to paraphrase Moses' message, it would go something like this: "If you're going to make these truths stick in the hearts of kids, you'll have to be more deliberate about moving to the rhythm. In the future, there will be things that distract you. But if you make faith a part of the rhythm of your life, it will be a priority for you and for the generations to come."

The Israelites who listened to Moses that day understood something about having God in the rhythm of life. As they wandered in the desert, they ate manna every morning. They followed a cloud of smoke during the day and a pillar of fire at night. But in Canaan, it would be harder to remember. Moses, like a good leader, looked into the future. In a land flowing with milk and honey, he knew they would no longer be dependent on manna. The rhythm of their lives was changing, and he knew they would have to be more deliberate about keeping God in the day-to-day moments.

Moses knew something we think is essential for you to remember as you improve your structure to make relationships matter.

When you make faith a part of the rhythms of life,
it becomes more fluid, more natural, and more everyday.

---

4. Deuteronomy 6:6-9, NIV

That's why we encourage every SGL to . . .
invite themselves over for a nightly dinner in the home of their second graders.
show up to tuck in their four-year-olds at night.
surprise their middle schoolers (and family) by cooking breakfast on a Saturday morning.

Just kidding. That could get a little weird. Actually, that's why we think it's so important for your ministry—and your SGLs—to partner with families.

We think two things are true:
No one will influence a kid more than a parent.
A parent isn't the only influence a kid needs.

If you want to have a significant impact in the life of a kid, you should influence two types of people: parents and small group leaders. Of course kids will have other adult influences in their life—and that's a good thing. But when you can influence parents and SGLs who are a part of a kid's "everyday" rhythm of life, you stand a better chance of giving them an "everyday" kind of faith.

The best way to leverage parents and SGLs is to synchronize their efforts. We say it all the time: Two combined influences have a greater impact than just two influences. When you get SGLs and parents on the same page, you significantly increase your influence in a kid's life. That's the power of synergy. It's the magic of repetition. Children learn best through routine. So, when families and SGLs move to the same rhythm, it helps accentuate learning and development.

The more people in a kid's life who are moving to the same rhythm, the greater the impact. The more you cooperate with the way life naturally happens, the more integrated faith will become.

> **We say it all the time: Two combined influences have a greater impact than just two influences.**

Moses recognized the danger of a compartmentalized faith. He anticipated the people's tendency to segment God into an isolated category instead of viewing Him as the integrating force that influences all of life. It's characteristic of humans to create an image of God that's so narrowly defined it separates Him completely from culture. Instead of seeing everything as connected to God's story, we love to categorize and segment our faith.

But notice Moses never said, "For the sake of our faith, maybe we should stay isolated in the wilderness. Our faith is safer here." Instead, he pushed ahead to invade Canaan with a plan. What he handed the Israelites that day was a strategy to create a rhythm that would help keep their faith alive. It was a rhythm that would break down the walls of every culture to reveal a God whose story transcends time and space.

And it was effective. Years later, the psalmist recorded something remarkable.

He [God] decreed statutes for Jacob and established the law in Israel, which He commanded our ancestors to teach their children, so the next generation would know them, even the children yet to be born, and they in turn would tell their children. Then they would put their trust in God and would not forget His deeds but would keep His commands.[5]

Generations later, after the conquest of Canaan, after the period of the judges, after the rise of the monarchy, the Israelites had a faith that was anchored to the God who led them through the wilderness. They still told the stories. They still remembered. They wrote it out in psalms. Why? Because they had the kind of everyday faith that stands the test of time.

When faith is something that only happens in church, it doesn't integrate into everyday life, and it fades. We've heard all the arguments for why the church should resist culture, and we know there's something about following Jesus that will change the way you live. Sure, your life will look different from the life of an unbeliever. But that doesn't mean you move to an entirely different rhythm. As a general rule, you shouldn't make culture your enemy.

---

5. Psalm 78:5-7, NIV

That is, as long as
you speak with language,
you play music,
you use air conditioning,
and kids wear clothes to church,
you will always do ministry within the context of culture.

But if you're smart, you can leverage the natural rhythms of culture to give kids an everyday faith. You can move to the rhythm that parents and SGLs are already programmed to move to. You can create a ministry that cooperates with the rhythm of the everyday.

It works with the seasons of the year.
It adjusts to the seasons of a kid's life.
It cooperates with the seasons of relationships.

The rhythm of your ministry is a structure issue. The way you organize your calendar, the way you leverage time, has the potential to support crucial relationships. So, create a structure for your small groups that moves to the rhythm.

Small groups should move to the rhythm by . . .
COOPERATING WITH THE PATTERNS OF THE TYPICAL YEAR.

There are natural rhythms to a year. The seasons come and go—or if you live in Muleshoe, Texas, the season just comes, and it stays. There's a time to reap, a time to sow, and a time to board up your windows if you live in Florida in early September.

If you're creating a ministry that moves to the rhythm in order to give kids an everyday faith, you need to consider the natural rhythms of the year.

The calendar has a rhythm.

Regardless of your theology about holidays, the kids and parents and SGLs in your community care about:

Valentine's Day
St. Patrick's Day
Easter
Labor Day
Halloween
Thanksgiving
Christmas
New School Year's Eve

That doesn't mean you have to create a program for every holiday, but it does mean you should think about them. Every holiday has a feel to it. Have you ever wondered why storefronts change their window displays or why sitcoms will have a "Valentine" episode or why Starbucks doesn't offer their best-selling pumpkin spice latte year-round? They're tapping into the rhythm of the year. They're leveraging the calendar.

So, here's a question. How do you leverage the calendar year to strengthen group?

THINK SCOPE AND CYCLE.

One way should be with your message. We think every ministry should have a scope and cycle for their content that cooperates with the rhythm of the year.

Scope: A comprehensive plan that prioritizes what you teach.

Cycle: Your plan to re-visit and reinforce what you teach, so it's effective.

Some educators use the term "sequence" instead of "cycle." But sequential learning is more effective with concepts that build in a linear fashion. First you learn to count, then you learn addition, then multiplication, then pre-algebra, then quantum physics. Once you master a concept, then you're ready to move on to something more complex.

Thinking in terms of sequential learning can be misleading when it comes to faith development unless you . . .
learn everything you need to know the first time.
immediately and forever apply every sermon after you hear it.
never discover something new in a passage of Scripture you've heard or read before.

When you think in terms of cyclical learning, you recognize core truths will have fresh meaning with every new life stage. Your scope prioritizes what you'll teach, and your cycle strategically recycles those principles again and again. There's something about repeating what matters that helps it stick. So, as you move to the rhythm of the year, your core message should be repeated in moments when it can connect most. If you're going to talk to preschoolers about how God made the world, why not do it in the spring when school is talking about Earth Day and their parents are taking them to the park? If you're going to talk to elementary kids about having respect for authority, why not do it at the beginning of the school year when they're introduced to new authority figures who will be with them every day? If you're going to talk to teenagers about moral purity, why not do it in February or March before Spring Break, Prom, and swimsuit season?

When you leverage the rhythm of the calendar, you partner with parents and small group leaders, because you communicate a message that works with the natural rhythm of life.

YOUR COMMUNITY HAS A RHYTHM.

While some holidays and seasons are universal, some patterns in the year are unique to your specific community. Whether it's the Pecos, Texas, rodeo in June, the Memphis, Tennessee, music festival in May, or the Chandler, Arizona, ostrich festival in March, you probably have some community events that are a part of the rhythm of your year.

You can either intentionally align your calendar to move with the rhythm of your community, or you can ignore it. But if you ignore the rhythm of your community, you'll have a hard time aligning parents and SGLs because—guess what?—they live in your community.

So, when it's hockey season, or the fair comes to town, or American Idol decides to host auditions right in your backyard, use it. Embrace it. Leverage it.

Also, sometimes the best way to embrace the rhythms of your community is to take a break.

Kevin Ragsdale told us, "We've chosen not to do student programming on Spring Break, Easter, Mothers' Day, Memorial Day, Labor Day, and two weeks at Christmas."

If you've read that list and now suspect Kevin is a heretic, don't worry. It's not because Kevin hates those holidays or what they represent. Actually, he's saying that he wants his small groups to cooperate with the home. That means when there's a significant event that can be leveraged best by a parent, he doesn't want to compete. His groups move to a rhythm that complements what happens at home.

YOUR MINISTRY HAS A RHYTHM.

The rest of your community might not be aware, but you probably have some rhythms that have become part of your church culture. Maybe it's a summer camp, a giving campaign, a church-wide emphasis on service, a family experience, a Christmas program, or an annual chili cook-off.

Whatever rhythms are a part of your church calendar, you can and should evaluate how they work to support groups.

Another friend of ours, Bobbi Miller, served at Willow Creek Community Church near Chicago and Bent Tree Bible Fellowship near Dallas. She told us that their student teams go on mission trips in the month of June, which she leveraged to support volunteer growth in her children's ministry. She said, "In July our elementary programming is staffed largely by our students who have just returned from their trips. They're excited and we take advantage of that, showing them that there's a mission field in their own church with the elementary kids. They do a tremendous job and many of them will plug in and serve in the fall."

One of the most significant rhythms of your ministry may be your trends in attendance. If you're like most of the ministries we talk to, your attendance patterns look something like this:

83

Your patterns may look different, but the point is the same. You should move to the rhythm of your ministry attendance patterns. How are you scheduling so groups can make the most of high attendance seasons? How are you anticipating low attendance months and planning accordingly?

SUMMERTIME

Let's talk about the summer. Most staff who work with small group ministries have some opinions about what to do with the summer. It's low attendance. Families go on vacation. SGLs go on vacation. It's sunny outside, and people just don't want to spend the morning inside. So, do your small groups continue to meet?

We don't have an answer for you. You'll have to decide. What we can say is this: Many children's ministries make a decision to use video-driven curriculum in order to give their production teams some time off. Some also discontinue small groups in order to let their leaders have more time with their own families. In most middle school and high school ministries though, the summer is a critical time for small groups to strengthen their connection. Students need leaders who can go to camp with them and make the most of their summer vacation.

However you decide to structure your groups, just remember they should complement, and not compete, with the attendance patterns in your ministry. When you cooperate with the rhythms of the year, you align parents and SGLs to incorporate faith into everyday life.

Small groups should move to the rhythm by . . .
CONSIDERING THE LIFECYCLE OF THE AVERAGE GROUP.

Just like every Tupperware-enclosed leftover in your ministry fridge, every group has a lifecycle.

When you're improving a structure that supports groups, it's important to consider how groups change. Each phase of a group presents unique opportunities and challenges. And when you understand what those are, you can move to the rhythm of the group.

EVERY GROUP HAS A BEGINNING.

The beginning of a group, like the beginning of a new friendship, is full of discovery. It can be exciting. It can also make some people a little uncomfortable. When you consider the lifecycle of your groups, you know what happens during the first group experiences matters more. Kids are getting a first impression of each other and of their leader. So, ask yourself this question: What can our ministry do to facilitate positive introductions during the first weeks of a group's time together?

Here's a basic principle to consider: The older the kid, the longer it will take for SGLs to build credibility and small groups to establish a connection. A preschooler trusts their SGL simply because they're a big person. As kids get older, SGLs have to earn their trust. So, as you build your scope and cycle, you might not want to have your middle school sex talk three weeks into a new year.

Some groups change in the middle of the year.
Every group has a unique story. There may be times an SGL moves away, a group loses momentum, or a group grows so fast you have to find a way to divide. When a group goes through a mid-cycle transition, whatever it is, there are a few things you can do to help make the transition smooth.

1. **PLAN FOR IT.** If the kids in your groups only know one adult, it will be hard for them to transition to someone else. Whether it's a coach, an apprentice, or the greeters in your hallways, who are you strategically positioning to take a group if an SGL leaves or a group divides?

2. **OVER-COMMUNICATE.** If the parents in your ministry have caught your vision for groups, they'll care when a group changes. It's important to let parents know as early as possible. Don't let their kid be the first one to communicate when a change has happened. You move first, and give them time to ask questions.

3. **MOVE SLOWLY WHEN POSSIBLE.** When a group grows, and grows, and grows, you'll eventually have to make a decision to divide the group. If you want every kid to be known, they can't stay in a group of thirty. That's not a small group. If you haven't already done so, introduce a new SGL to co-lead the group. Give the group time to connect. Let the two SGLs work with you to divide the list of kids and come up with a plan for their transition. Let the leaders spend a few weeks connecting with the kids who will be on their list—just to connect. Then make an announcement to the group.

4. **CONSIDER THE SEASON.** If you know you're going to ask a leader to leave, it's better to do it before student camp than after. If you know a group needs to divide, it's better to split them in January then right at Christmas. Whenever you make a change, consider the rhythm of a year and the season of the group, so you can select a time that works.

5. **STAY POSITIVE.** Change is hard. When groups encounter change mid-cycle, you'll probably encounter pushback from parents or kids or both. You can and should listen to their concerns. But stay positive. Sometimes change is the best thing for a group.

EVERY GROUP HAS AN END.

As much as we think consistency is essential for a healthy small group culture, we think kids *should* have more than one small group experience as they move through various age-group ministries. It's not that group relationships formed in preschool won't last beyond kindergarten, but small groups shouldn't. No SGL should stay with a group from birth to graduation—that's one

reason kids have parents. There are seasons for kids and seasons
for groups.

Actually, research shows that kids who have five or more adults
who invest in their faith over time have a greater chance of having
a mobilized faith. So, when you create a small group culture, you
give kids someone—again and again. You give them multiple
adults as they move through your family ministry from birth
through graduation because you anchor their personal faith to a
community of faith.

As a group ends, remember that you're helping kids and families
move from one life-stage to another as smoothly as possible.
Here's one important principle: The older the kid, the longer
the transition will take. This is especially true when you're
transitioning someone from one age group ministry to the next.
We think it might go something like this:

Four-year-olds into kindergarten—one month
Fifth grade into middle school ministry—two months
Eighth grade into high school ministry—three months
Seniors into whatever comes next—one year

TRANSITIONING SENIORS
Several years ago, I (Kristen) led a group of senior girls. As May
drew near, I remember having mixed emotions. Even though
the church celebrated our group with a graduation dinner and
handed me a gift card as a sign of gratitude for the past four
years, I couldn't help but feel that my time with this group was
incomplete. It felt like I was letting go, just when they were
leaning in.

After talking with the youth minister at my church, I decided to
commit to an extra year with my group. My goal was simple. I
didn't want to let go until they were connected to someone else. I

knew college was a critical transition, and I didn't want them to navigate it alone.

Some of the girls were planning to live at home and get a job after graduation. Some went to local state universities, and others moved away to universities around the country. Their first semester, I visited each of the college campuses that was within driving distance; I went on a weekend so we could attend a church near their campus together. I set up a day each week to send messages on Facebook (since that's where they connected best at the time). When the girls were home for holidays, I planned a Christmas party and sleepover.

A lot of what I did that year was both systematic and organic. Each girl experienced transition in her own unique way, so the amount of time I spent with each individual wasn't equal. But for most, our relationship went deeper in that one year than it had in the four years prior. The challenges they faced were more significant. The decisions they had to make held greater weight. By the end of that year, I was more convinced than ever that graduates need more than a Sunday celebration to transition into the next stage of life.

Now I remind church leaders every time I get the chance that high school graduation should not be viewed as a finish line, but another critical transition. Remember this:

Don't disconnect when the stakes are the highest.
Instead, tap into your relational influence when the felt need is the greatest.

Whether you're transitioning seniors to college, fifth graders to middle school, or four-year-olds to kindergarten, transitioning effectively takes time.

It also takes connection. Remember, if you're creating a culture where parents and SGLs work together to impact the everyday faith of a kid, you have to get them on the same page. Transitions give you a unique opportunity to get your parents and SGLs together—in the same room—to share something that will help them navigate the year ahead with success.

Think about it this way. Whenever a kid transitions, you can do two things:
Give parents and leaders helpful information related to their kid's stage of life.
Connect parents with SGLs so they know they have someone on their team.

When you align parents and SGLs, you mobilize two influences to have a greater combined impact in the life of a kid. If you want to fight for everyday, authentic faith in the next generation, you need to support the relationships that matter most. You need to move to the rhythm.

When you get in the habit of moving to the rhythm, you cooperate with what's already happening so groups happen better.

EMPOWER LEADERS

WHO MAKE

RELATIONSHIPS MATTER.

That's because the depth of relationships is determined by your investment in leaders.

It's just a wild guess.

Maybe we've got you all wrong.

But we think maybe . . . just *maybe* . . .

You got into ministry because
you care about kids.
You believe kids are capable
of really big things.
You want kids to know and love God.
And you probably even like spending time
with them. (You know, most of the time.)

And since you care about kids, and you know the best way to help a kid know God is to give them someone who knows God, maybe you went into ministry because you thought that person could be you.

But here's the thing. That person can't be you.

At least, you can't be that person for every kid. Your capacity is limited.

Think about it. Between your family and personal friends, you've already used up a lot of your relational capacity. If you try to add 20, 30, maybe 100 kids to the mix, you're going to forget or miss some of the critical elements that connect you to them. Your influence is built on those connections.

Birthdays.
Ballgames.
Background stories.

These form the foundation of the relationships you're building and one person, not even you, can build them all. This is why we *need* other intentional adults to join us in the process. We need small group leaders.

So, if you want to influence the next generation, it's not enough that you care about kids. You need to care about adults, too. Leveraging your relational capacity to care for and about a group of well-trained adults who are passionate about investing in the lives of kids can increase your impact exponentially.

If your answer for discipleship is small group,
and the primary place you want a kid to be is small group,
then small group leaders are your most important volunteers.

> **If your answer for discipleship is small group, and the primary place you want a kid to be is small group, then small group leaders are your most important volunteers.**

This group of adult leaders represents your biggest opportunity. And as Jim Collins told us in *Good to Great*, "Put your best people on your biggest opportunity." We believe your small group leaders are your best volunteers, and the potential that small groups hold is your biggest opportunity. Not to just develop a group of leaders, but to shape a group of pastors.

Not . . .
volunteers
helpers
chaperones
babysitters
teachers
discussion-leaders or
chaos-managers.

Pastors.

I (Shef) can't count the number of times that I've arrived at a hurting kid's house only to find their "pastor" already there. One time in particular stands out when the father of a student had taken his own life. I was walking into a situation where there were questions no one is prepared to answer. The only thing you bring is love and understanding. When I arrived, there was his small group leader, with his arm around him, loving and understanding him in a way that no one person can provide for dozens of kids. My job was to support that leader in his role as a pastor, and it was an honor to do it.

If you believe the depth of relationships is determined by your investment in leaders, it should motivate you to empower the leader so they can lead.

This is something Kevin Ragsdale has been saying to North Point small group leaders for years. "When I first started ministry," Kevin told us, "I realized I couldn't create a great ministry experience if I tried to be the student pastor to all of our students." Knowing North Point's student ministry would quickly grow beyond the reach of his own capacity, Kevin empowered his SGLs to be the pastors of their small groups.

One pastor might not be enough to disciple every kid in your ministry, but what if instead of just one pastor your ministry could have 15? 30? 100? Can you imagine the experience every kid could have if her pastor knew her name? If his pastor knew his struggles at home? If their pastor could truly pastor?

But let's pause here for a second. Maybe you're not sure about this idea.

Maybe you're thinking, *But isn't pastoring and discipling **my** job, not theirs?*

Well . . . no.

When Jesus commanded us to go and make disciples, there weren't any pastors in the crowd. There were fishermen, farmers, a tax collector or two, but no pastors. Just passionate followers of a Man who entrusted this important work to regular people. The same kind of people who fill our hallways and auditoriums every week.

But, "I've been to seminary and they haven't been trained." Then train them. "But I get paid to pastor them." Then pastor more of them for the same pay. That's not just what Jesus would do—it's what He did.

Okay, maybe you're still a little nervous.

After all, who's to say they won't do things differently than you would? Say things differently? They probably will. Just remember. No matter how many steps you take, no matter how many parameters you set, you'll never be able to control everything that happens in small group. What you can do is, like Jesus, pour yourself into them and allow them to learn from you.

Isn't it true that Jesus took the same risks with you and me? Small group leaders won't get it right every time. But let's be honest. Neither will we.

What you can do is place the best people you can find into the lives of kids. And the next few pages are full of information on how to find, choose, and develop great small group leaders.

If you don't want to empower SGLs to disciple kids, that's okay. You don't have to. But if you don't, here's what's going to happen:

If you don't empower small group leaders, you will limit your influence to your own relational capacity. You may get to have great, focused influence on a few kids, but that's about it.

If you don't empower small group leaders, you will limit someone's perspective on God to your individual perspective on God. Your voice is important, but it's not the only voice kids need to hear.

If you don't empower small group leaders, you will limit the Church, and you will send the message to the kids and adults you influence that ministry is best left in the hands of the "professionals."

If you're okay with limiting your ministry, limiting someone's perspective on God, and limiting the Church, then don't empower small group leaders. Don't give away influence. Don't give away ministry.

But if you care about kids and want to help them have an authentic faith, then you can't do it alone. You don't have that kind of capacity. No one does. If you believe small groups are the answer, then you've got to empower leaders.

The best way to expand your influence is to empower leaders.

PRACTICE 1
EXPECT MORE, NOT LESS
(Let's talk about expectations.)

Let's see if we can read your mind right now. "If I can't get my leaders to show up for a meeting, how can I get them to be pastors?" Sound about right? These kind of leaders aren't a dime a dozen. They're incredibly valuable, and they're looking to invest in something valuable.

If you think it's impossible to find committed leaders, here's something to consider:

Maybe your leaders aren't committed because you haven't yet asked them to commit to something significant.

I (Kristen) led small groups for five years in a variety of settings: churches, para-church ministries, camps, as a volunteer, and as a staff intern. But for five years, no one ever asked me for a long-term weekly commitment. Instead, I was asked to lead for a summer, for a season, or for a school year. But the summer after my senior year of college, I interned at a ministry that raised the bar. When I offered to take a small group, they hesitated. (I had never seen a church hesitate about a volunteer before.) They wanted to make sure I understood that by taking a group for the summer, I wasn't just volunteering to see them through the summer, or the school year—but for four years. They didn't even want me to sign up for a group of freshmen if I wasn't going to make a commitment to be there on Graduation Sunday.

Seriously?

Yes. Seriously. The big commitment felt intimidating at first. But two, three, four years later I knew I would never lead another small group any other way. I was compelled to sign up again and again, and recruit others to do the same.

If you're looking for small group leaders who are up for a big challenge, you've got to make a big ask. If you want to empower your SGLs, then you've got to expect more, not less.

One of the greatest indicators your ministry is moving toward a relational culture is this: You have consistent leaders who show up in the lives of kids and students.

Sometimes we get questions about that last statement, so maybe we should clarify:
By consistent, we mean they're not rotational.
By not rotational, we mean they show up weekly.
By weekly, we mean they're there every week.

Of course, SGLs will miss some weeks. Honestly they probably should . . .
go on vacation from time to time.
stay home if they have the flu.
be present for family members even if it means skipping out on their group.

But for the most part, you're recruiting leaders who will make a weekly commitment to kids and teenagers.

"For how long?" you ask.

Well, that depends. Remember it takes preschoolers less time to connect with a leader than it will when they're in elementary. It takes middle school students and high school students even longer to establish a pattern of trust within their group and with their leader. That's why we think the commitment should be different for SGLs in different age groups.

> **Maybe your leaders aren't committed because you haven't yet asked them to commit to something significant.**

In most preschool and children's ministries, we encourage SGLs to stay with a group from 10 to 12 months, depending on how that ministry handles the summer.

In middle school, we encourage SGLs to stay with their group for two to three years, depending on how the ministry is structured.

In high school, we encourage SGLs to stay with their group for four to five years, in order to stay with a group of kids from freshman year through their first year of college.

If having committed weekly volunteers is a new concept for your ministry, we know transition takes time. In fact, we'll cover steps to transitioning to a small group culture at the end of the book. We know it's a big ask. But we believe the scope of your influence is determined by the success of your leaders. Which is why when you empower your leaders, you'll start by expecting more, not less.

Expect more not less, so
LEADERS KNOW THEY'RE DOING SOMETHING THAT MATTERS.

So, what do you want your leaders to do?

Hang on for just a second.

If you want committed SGLs, you can't begin with the what or even the how of leading groups. You've got to begin with *why?*

If you want leaders who are committed, they've got know their job matters. Sue Miller, the innovator responsible for making every week matter for kids at Willow Creek, reminds us, "No one wants to do something that's inconsequential."

It only takes a few moments on Instagram to confirm that the world is full of inconsequential opportunities. Never have there been more ways to waste our most valuable resource: time. And the kind of leader you're looking for doesn't waste their time. They invest it. Great leaders want to know what they do matters and it matters to you that they do it.

Could anything matter more than a kid getting a glimpse of the love of God through someone who loves God? We don't think so. And the leader who feels the responsibility for showing that kind of love won't either. But it's our job to empower them with that responsibility.

Not just responsibility for . . .
sorting the goldfish crackers
assisting with a craft
refereeing a game
disciplining disruptive behaviors.

But responsibility to . . .
know the details of a kid's world
connect with a kid's parents
show up for significant life events
answer tough questions
do the work of ministry.

If you want your small group leaders to know they're doing something that matters, give them a job that matters. Great leaders rise to a challenge.

But even if some don't rise to the challenge, that's okay. You don't need everyone to be an SGL. You just need the right people. (We'll talk more about finding and recruiting the right people a little bit later.) You need great SGLs who are ready for a big challenge because they understand how much it matters.

And they're out there. They're just waiting on someone to cast a vision big enough and valuable enough for them to give their time to.

Expect more not less so
LEADERS KNOW WHAT YOU WANT THEM TO DO.

When a potential small group leader shows up at your door, they're going to have two questions for you: "What do you want me to do?" And, "How do you want me to do it?"

For the past decade, we've been talking to ministry leaders around the country about creating a culture of small groups for kids and teenagers. In these conversations, one of the number-one questions leaders ask is, "What's the job of a small group leader?"

A few years ago, we set out to answer that question. For months, we met every Tuesday night to talk with small group leaders and church leaders from churches of all sizes, denominations, and demographics to clarify what a small group leader does, and what they need to know in order to succeed. The insights and conversations from those late-night meetings became a book called *Lead Small*.

Simply put, we think a small group leader is: "anyone who chooses to invest in the lives of a few to encourage authentic faith."

That's the definition.

If you want the full description, you're going to have to read *Lead Small*, but if we could just sum it up for you, it would look something like this:

Every SGL should do five things.

BE PRESENT
Connect their faith to a community.

Someone once asked me (Shef) which spiritual gifts I looked for in potential leaders. I told them I don't think there's any spiritual gift more important than the gift of showing up.

Yep. We were serious about that weekly thing. The first thing anyone must do if they want to be an SGL is show up. They need to show up predictably, weekly, in the lives of kids and teenagers so they can earn the kind of trust they need if they want to impact a kid's faith.

They also need to show up mentally. They need to be fully present with their few while they're with them. Which probably means you should send SGLs their weekly small group materials in advance. That way, they aren't trying to read while they manage their group.

And they need to show up randomly. SGLs need to practice being present outside the regularly scheduled, come-to-church-to-see-me times. Whether it's a card in the mail or a sign and an air horn at the Friday night football game, SGLs have a greater connection with their few when they show up for them in unexpected ways.

CREATE A SAFE PLACE
Clarify their faith as they grow.

Small groups are messy. Anytime you put a group of kids or teenagers together in a room, with all their differences, all their personalities, and all their preferences, there's going to be some tension. But the way SGLs manage that tension has the potential to create a place that's safe enough for kids to authentically process faith.

If leaders want to create a safe place, they have to lead the group. Every group needs a leader who isn't a peer. (That's why we don't advocate for student-led student groups.) Every group needs someone to lead, so the group will value things like acceptance, confidentiality, and honesty.

If leaders want to make their group a safe place, they also have to respect the process. They have to understand that God is at work in every kid's life in a way that may take a little time.

Leaders who create safe places also guard the heart. Some things kids share in group cannot be kept confidential. We think there are three basic reasons an SGL should break confidentiality: When a kid is hurting themselves. When a kid is hurting someone else. When a kid is being hurt.

Your ministry should have clear and specific guidelines for when and how an SGL breaks confidentiality. Communicate your expectations regularly. An SGL who guards the heart of a kid ensures that kid is physically and emotionally safe, both in the group and out of it.

PARTNER WITH PARENTS
Nurture an everyday faith.

This may be one of the most challenging lead small principles. Most SGLs sign up because they want to help kids or teenagers— not their parents. But remember two things we said are true: No one has more potential to influence a kid than a parent. And every parent wants to be a better parent. So if SGLs want to make a lasting impact on the everyday faith of a kid, they have to partner with parents.

An SGL should cue the parent with information that will prompt a parent to do more than they might otherwise do. That probably means you, the church leader, should cue your SGLs so they can cue parents.

An SGL should also honor the parent in the way they talk to and about parents with their few. We tell SGLs all the time, "Never use their relational tension for your relational gain." Train your leaders to model an attitude of respect for parents in front of those they lead.

And finally, an SGL should reinforce the family by always valuing and not competing with the family for the kid's time, attention, and affection. If you're going to create a rhythm in your ministry that reinforces the family, make sure your SGLs have the same philosophy when it comes to significant milestones and group outings.

MAKE IT PERSONAL
Inspire their faith by your example.

When SGLs invest in a few, their few have a front row seat to their lives. Did that make your heart skip a beat or two? Of course it did. If you're tempted to install software to monitor the Facebook profiles and Instagram images of your SGLs, or if you're wanting to make every leader keep a record of their prayer life to submit to you monthly, it's probably because you understand the power of their example.

You can't control the spiritual habits of your leaders, but you can remind them of the importance of making it personal. If you want leaders to make it personal, you should help them live in community. Every SGL needs a group of peers that isn't their group of first graders.

If you want leaders to make it personal, you should help them set priorities. We're not just saying to help them prioritize their few, but to help them have personal and spiritual priorities that will give them the kind of personal health to lead well.

If you want leaders to make it personal, you should give them permission to be real. Not *too* real. Third graders probably don't need to hear about their SGLs latest breakup—in detail. They need a leader who can be authentic about . . .
their love of pimento cheese sandwiches
their lack of knowledge about hip Indie bands
their struggles and discoveries about faith.

One more note about setting priorities and being real: In a world filled with social media sites, your leaders are bound to share a lot of very real stuff outside the walls of your ministry that parents and kids in your ministry can see. When you set expectations for your SGLs, you may want to cover a few ground rules about their online presence. Otherwise, last week's spring break tattoo may become a very significant part of this week's small group conversation.

MOVE THEM OUT
Engage their faith in a bigger story.

Small group leaders should know that what happens inside their circle will always be measured by what happens outside the circle. An SGL has significant influence in the life of a kid, but they aren't the only influence a kid needs. That's why, when it comes to their kids and teenagers, your SGLs need to move them to someone else.

Discipleship happens best when there's an experiential component. Especially as kids get older, they'll discover more about God while they're doing what God wants them to do than they will while sitting in a circle talking about ideas. That's why SGLs need to look for ways to plug their few in to serve and move them to be the Church.

Eventually, every group ends. Leaders take new groups, and kids grow up and move on. But when you have committed SGLs, they aren't content just to let their kids go. They want to make sure their few transition well. They want to help move them to what's next.

There's nothing especially remarkable about the five characteristics of *Lead Small*. They just simplify a few things so they're easier to talk about. The phrases act as a starting point, since everything you need to train your SGLs to do can fall into these five categories. They give you and your team a common language, so you're all on the same page. They clarify the values and expectations you have for your SGLs.

If this whole lead small thing is new to you, you might be looking at these characteristics thinking, *That's really asking a **lot** from a volunteer.* Yes. It is. That's what *expecting more, not less* is all about.

When you expect more from your SGLs, you have to be clear about what you expect them to do. Giving them a job description is great, but it's not something you can hand to an SGL one time and be done. We'll talk much more about training in the next chapter, but when it comes to letting an SGL know what you want them to do, remember: You need to say it clearly. You need to say it well. And you need to say it more than once.

"The greatest challenge for our staff has been inspiring and equipping our leaders on a wide scale," said Gina McClain, co-author of *Don't Quit: The Best Things in Ministry Come Over Time*. "That level of vision casting requires constantly weaving the vision of lead small into every available avenue of communication."

Every fall, we have an opportunity to travel to different cities to talk with church leaders. After we wrote *Lead Small*, we were telling a room full of leaders about these five ideas. At the end of the message a lady came up to talk to me (Reggie), and she was emotional. She had been a small group leader for 50 years. Can you imagine! This woman had given her life to investing in kids to help them develop an authentic faith. When she heard this message she said, "I've been doing this for 50 years. I just never understood what I was doing until now."

When you help a leader know what they do,
you prepare them to do it.
you motivate them to do it better.
you inspire them to keep doing it.

Expect more not less, so
LEADERS KNOW YOU BELIEVE THEY CAN DO IT.

Once you've given your leaders a job that matters and told them how to do it, can you guess what's next? Yep. You *let them do it*. Because until you step away and let them do it, they'll never believe *you* believe they can do it.

Let's go back to the Great Commission again. After Jesus gave us our mission, do you remember what happened? Sure you do. *He left*—at least physically. He stepped back. He let the disciples do what He asked them to do. There's something about the ascension that communicates just how much Jesus entrusts to those who follow Him. He believed the Gospel would spread, disciples would be made, and the Church would move forward—by people like you and me.

In the same way, if you want empowered leaders, you need to take a giant step back and let them do what you've asked them to do.

Jesus doesn't shake His head in disbelief if we get the wrong font on the monthly posters, or load the wrong live lyrics into the computer. He doesn't throw up His hands in frustration and say, "Forget it, I'll take care of it," when He notices a small group has erupted into a spontaneous cheese-ball fight instead of engaging in meaningful conversation. No, Jesus entrusted His disciples with a great mission, and then left them with a surprising amount of free will and authority to pull the whole thing off.

Of course, He is God. And He did send His Spirit. At the end of the day, everything is ultimately in His control. We aren't really suggesting the mission and ministry of the church is completely run by people. Neither are we suggesting that you let your kindergarten SGLs run their group like a private club. They're still responsible to you and your ministry team.

We're just suggesting there will be moments when . . .
you become less of a big deal, so small group leaders can be a bigger deal.
you take less responsibility, so they can do something that matters.
you don't solve the problem because you know they're capable on their own.

If your small group leaders are going to believe they can do it, they've got to know *you* believe they can do it. And they'll never know *you* believe they can do it until you actually *let* them do it.

When you get in the habit of expecting more from your small group leaders,
your small group leaders will lead in ways you never expected.

PRACTICE 2
PLAY FAVORITES
(Let's talk about training.)

Teachers probably shouldn't play favorites with their students. Parents probably shouldn't play favorites with their kids. But if you want to empower leaders, you've got to play favorites with your small group leaders.

Jesus certainly played favorites. Remember Peter, James, and John? Enough said.

Whether you realize it or not, you *already* play favorites in other areas of your life. Don't believe it? When you plan a party, do you open your Contacts file and start with the A's? We didn't think so. You go to your . . . wait for it . . . *favorites*. Even your iPhone understands this.

Still not convinced? Okay, think about this: How many Facebook friends do you have? The average adult has around 338. (Yes, we looked it up.) So, let's say you're average. Start naming them. All 338. We'll wait.

First of all, it's okay that you can't name all 338 of your Facebook friends. This doesn't make you a terrible friend because, as you might recall, your capacity is limited. You can't possibly be expected to have quality relationships with 338 people. And secondly, it really is okay to play favorites.

"But not with volunteers right? I mean they're volunteers." Yes, even with volunteers.

Remember all the volunteers we said you have? There are some who . . .
welcome kids at the door.
help families register and sign in.
keep your area safe.
run your production.
feed everyone.
lead small groups.

Regardless of the size of your ministry, you probably have some
volunteers who help you make your weekly environments happen.
We know you appreciate every single one of those volunteers.
But while all volunteers are important, your small group leaders
should be your favorites. They're your inner circle.

Remember, your relational capacity is around eight to 10 people.
And just like you don't have the capacity to invest in every kid, you
might not have the capacity to equally invest in every volunteer. If
you have more than eight volunteers on your team . . . (You know
where we're going with this, don't you?)

Once you've surpassed your relational capacity with your
volunteers, you can no longer . . .

know every name.
remember every birthday.
follow every story.
keep up with every need.
pastor every volunteer.

You need to prioritize your influence to focus on the volunteers
who matter most. You need to prioritize your SGLs because
there's simply more at stake with your SGLs. Their responsibility
is greatest because you've given them the most influence in kids'
lives. And because you're expecting the most from them, you've
got to give them more than you give any other volunteer.

More time.
More training.
More care.

Think of it this way: If you want your small group leaders to give kids a place to belong, then maybe you should go first by giving SGLs a place to belong. Just like your kids and students need "someone" your SGLs need "someone," too.

> **"**
>
> # If you want your small group leaders to give kids a place to belong, then maybe you should go first by giving SGLs a place to belong.

That's why you need someone who feels directly responsible for your SGLs. Let's call that person a coach.

Maybe that coach is you. Maybe it's not.
Maybe it's someone already on your team, or maybe it's someone you still need to find.
Maybe it's a staff person, or maybe it's a volunteer.
Maybe it's one person, or maybe it's several.

Regardless of the size and organization of your ministry, small group leaders need *someone* who prioritizes them. They need someone who gives them time, training, and care. They need someone who knows what's going on in their groups, and in their lives, too. They need a coach.

So, what is a *coach*?
A *coach* is someone who is responsible for managing and shepherding SGLs.

A COACH MANAGES. Small group leaders need a coach because they need someone to manage the details that go into creating a great small group experience.

SGLs need someone who . . .
knows when they show up.
monitors the size of their group.
thinks about the dynamics of their group.
provides the supplies they need to make group happen.

But managing can't be *all* a coach does. That model just won't work. It's not enough.

A COACH SHEPHERDS. Small group leaders don't just need someone to care about the management of their group. They need someone to care about *them*.

SGLs need someone who . . .
listens to their stories.
knows the name of their dog.
cares about their job changes, new babies, and big moves.
takes care of them before they show up to take care of kids.

The best model for a coach is a mixture of manager and shepherd. In our experience, the best coaches are 50 percent administrative and 50 percent relational. They manage details, and they care for people.

So, how many coaches do you need?

We're back to that relational capacity again. You can do the math. If you have six SGLs, maybe you incorporate coaching responsibilities as part of your or another staff member's job description. Or maybe you have someone you've recruited to serve in this capacity. If you have 15 small group leaders, you need to develop a coaching system. Recruit three coaches, and put someone in charge of those coaches.

It's a relational numbers game. We think the winning formula looks something like this . . .
8 leaders = 1 coach

But remember how you organize to be organic? This formula isn't mentioned anywhere in Acts, so if you have nine leaders to one coach it doesn't mean you aren't Biblical. Just discover what works best for your ministry.

So, what's your solution?
How can you arrange or rearrange your team to give your SGLs a coach?
Do you need to make a new hire? Do you need to recruit a new team of volunteers?

Unfortunately, we can't answer those questions for you. But we can tell you this: A great coaching strategy will meet three significant needs for your small group leaders.

And it starts with making a few lists . . .

When you play favorites,
YOUR SMALL GROUP LEADERS MAKE
IT ONTO YOUR SHORT LIST.

SGLs NEED TO BE KNOWN.

I (Kristen) began leading my second small group in the fall of 1999. Only a few weeks after moving 832 miles away from home to begin my freshman year of college, I found a local ministry and signed up to lead a small group. I was excited to do something that would matter and wanted to invest in the lives of a few. We met every Tuesday for a large group program and every Thursday after school for small group. We did book studies. We had small group parties. I went to their basketball games and got to know their parents. On the surface, anyone looking in would have said things were working well. But the problem was, I was on course for a major crash, and no one leading that ministry knew. As a student-athlete with a job and a small group, I had filled every hour of every day with one commitment after another. I hadn't yet found my own community or made time for friends. I felt more alone than ever. During one of our weekly large group environments, I remember looking around the room and thinking, *No one here knows me.* I knew them. I knew my few. But I wasn't truly known by anyone who I served with or served under.

Since one of the five roles of a small group leader is to "make it personal," someone on your ministry team should have the responsibility of knowing your SGLs personally. Your coaches don't have to be a marriage counselor, chemistry tutor, personal shopper, or party planner for your SGLs. Coaches don't have to spend long hours listening to the story of a best friend's, brother's, ex-fiancé's latest vacation. But they should know the leader in a way that's more than purely functional.

Let's put it this way: Someone should know your SGL
less than their therapist,
but more than their car mechanic.

When you play favorites,
YOUR SMALL GROUP LEADERS MAKE IT ONTO YOUR
WEEKLY TO-DO LIST.

SGLs NEED TO BE TRAINED.

Think for a minute about all the things you need to do every
week to make your environments happen and keep your
ministry moving.

Okay. Now, stop.

That's a long list! What if we said there are a few more things you
should add to your weekly to-do list? Things like . . .
giving SGLs their small group materials in advance,
casting and recasting vision to SGLs,
cueing SGLs to connect with their few,
training SGLs so they can be better at what they do.

Coaching SGLs takes time. SGLs don't just need to be known, they
need to know what they need to know.

If the idea of training SGLs causes you to break out in a sweat as
visions of three-ring binders and syllabi flash through your mind,
take heart. Never has training been so easy or so available. Thanks
to the internet, training is only a click away and much of it is free.

Email, texting, social media, blogs, and video-sharing sites have
revolutionized the way we communicate with each other. So
there's no need to cram countless training sessions on to your
calendar. Of course, you can decide how best to train your SGLs—
we just know you should train them.

Train your SGLs annually.

Each year, you have one good opportunity to bring SGLs together for an official "kick-off." But have you ever noticed how difficult it is to plan an event that pleases *everyone?* Some come because they want to be inspired. Some come looking for a date. Others come for the food. How do you plan a training event that connects with as many people as possible? Here's a simple formula we've found to be effective:

1/3 Connection + 1/3 Information +1/3 Inspiration . . .
And always have food.

Connection
No small group leader should lead alone. They need to know you and your staff. They need to know each other. They need to know that leading a small group is sometimes a team effort. So, if you plan an annual event to kick-off the year, plan a little time for them to connect.

Information
There are probably some logistical things you'll want your leaders to know about you, about your ministry, and about your church. They need to know where to go, what to wear, how to sign in. If they work in the toddler room, they may need to know which bathroom to use. Don't spend time going over everything you want them to know. No one likes showing up for a meeting just to hear what you could have sent in an email. But take the time you need to answer their questions and give them the information they need to be successful.

Inspiration
You've made a big ask of your SGLs. If you want them to know they have a significant role in your ministry, now is one—of many—times to tell them. Inspire your leaders to be present, create a safe place, partner with parents, make it personal, and

move them out. Tell stories. Show videos. Make a really big deal about what they're about to do for the kids in their group.

Here's something you might want to consider: Toddlers aren't the same as teenagers. Wait, you already knew that. So, when you inspire SGLs, consider making it specific for the age group they'll work with this year. We believe SGLs who work with preschoolers can do something remarkable for kids at that age that's unique to that phase of life. The same is true for elementary, middle school, and high school. SGLs at each age group have a unique role to play. Sometimes we say it this way:

Preschool
EMBRACE their physical needs to know God's love and meet God's family.

Elementary
ENGAGE their interests to trust God's character and experience God's family.

Middle school
AFFIRM their personal journey to own their faith and value a faith community.

High school
MOBILIZE their potential to keep pursuing authentic faith and discover a personal ministry.

You can put your own spin on it. Just remember to let your leaders know *why* what they do is a significant part of your ministry. Use your annual "kick-off" event to inspire them with language you'll continue to use throughout the year. This is the set-up. Everything that comes after will be how you reinforce what matters again and again.

Train your SGLs seasonally.
No matter how well you inspire leaders at your "kick-off" event, there's a good chance the inspiration will fade over time—like maybe by next week. Just like you have a scope and cycle for the kids in your ministry, you probably need a cycle to help you train and inspire your leaders on a regular basis. Think about the natural rhythm and flow of the year. As you train your leaders, you should have a monthly focus that corresponds to those natural rhythms. We came up with one example of what a seasonal training plan for SGLs might look like:

August – 5 Principles of Lead Small
September – Create a Safe Place
October – Move Them Out (to serve)
November – Special Event
December – Partner with Parents
January – Make It Personal
February – Create a Safe Place
March – Be Present
April – Partner with Parents
May – Move Them Out (to what's next)
June – Make It Personal
July – Be Present

One way to leverage the calendar in training your SGLs is through special events. When you have a camp or retreat coming up, your SGLs will feel the tension of being prepared for that event. If you schedule a training before the event, you'll increase the likelihood of attendance as well as have everyone's attention. This is especially true if there's a Gospel presentation at the event and SGLs know that they may be answering questions about a kid's decision to follow Christ.

121

Train your SGLs weekly.
You can and should do something every week to train your SGLs. Whoever is responsible for your leaders should have a weekly to-do list that looks something like this:
- **Monday:** Write and mail an SGL a note.
- **Tuesday:** Take an SGL out for coffee.
- **Wednesday:** Post about your monthly series to Instagram.
- **Thursday:** Send all SGLs a weekly email.
- **Saturday:** Text SGLs important information.
- **Sunday:** Brag about groups publicly on Facebook, Instagram, and Twitter.

Every time you send small group curriculum or discussion guides, write an email, post to social media, text, or connect with your SGLs in any way, you have an opportunity to train them in bite-sized pieces. There are countless, simple things you can do every week to give your leaders the tools and knowledge they need to help them be better small group leaders.

We actually created an entire website, hired a team of people, and produce new content every single week that does exactly what we just outlined. Need an easy-to-check-off-because-we-already-did-it-for-you to-do list? Try a subscription to Weekly at GoWeekly.com.

When you play favorites,
YOUR SMALL GROUP LEADERS MAKE
IT ONTO YOUR PARTY LIST.

SGLs NEED TO BE CELEBRATED.
There's a principle that says, "Reward what you want repeated." So if you want your SGLs to repeat what they do year after year, you have to find a way to reward them—to celebrate them. Oh sure, you celebrate a lot of things. Maybe you celebrated the number of

kids baptized last month, or the amount of canned goods collected for the community food drive, or that only one kid got hit in the face at the dodge ball tournament. You've probably celebrated some great things recently. But how often do you celebrate your SGLs?

Remember, these are your favorites. These are the best and brightest leaders you have and they're worth celebrating. If you ever doubt that, think about how hard they'd be to replace. That's what determines the value of something—the cost it takes to replace it. The hours of searching, training, and development it takes to get an SGL to where he or she needs to be is sizable. Isn't it worth celebrating them if it helps you to hang on to them?

A great coach prioritizes the celebration of small group leaders because small group leaders are worth throwing parties for.

Celebrate them publicly.

Look for every opportunity you can to celebrate your SGLs publicly—your church program, in staff meetings, in front of parents, to other SGLs, in front of kids, and online. When you're making an announcement about upcoming camps or an upcoming series your family ministry is doing, thank a couple of SGLs. When your kids are baptized, when you can, have them name and thank their SGL for the role they played in their spiritual journey. Celebrate the leaders who are doing it well by spotlighting their stories. Let the vision spread by their example.

Celebrate them privately.

When you see an SGL do something great, acknowledge it with a handwritten note, a quick email, or a compliment in the hallway. (In a day of text messaging and email, there's nothing quite like a hand-written thank-you note.) The only thing better would be a bag of thank-you notes from the parents of the kids you lead in small group. A few weeks before a big event involving your SGLs, try emailing the parents of each group and ask them to write a note thanking the leaders for their investment.

Celebrate them randomly.
Whether it's birthdays, anniversaries, holidays, end-of-the-year appreciations, or just because, create opportunities to celebrate small group leaders unexpectedly and randomly. Remember, being an SGL is a big job. That unexpected celebration might be just what they need the moment they need it.

When you get in the habit of coaching SGLs by playing favorites, you're doing for them what you're asking them to do for their few.

WIN BEFORE YOU BEGIN
(Let's talk about recruitment.)

I magine for a moment you're back in high school gym class . . . during the dodgeball unit. You pull on the t-shirt and mesh shorts you probably haven't washed since August, tie your shoelaces tight, and jog toward the basketball courts where your physical education teacher is waiting. He says he's going to "randomly" appoint two team captains, but since his selections are this year's starting quarterback for the football team and a far-less-celebrated Rubik's Cube aficionado wearing a fedora, you suspect your gym teacher may be mistaken about the definition of random.

Team selections begin.
QB drafts one of his teammates—an offensive lineman.
Fedora drafts his buddy from the debate team.
QB picks his girlfriend—starting pitcher for the girl's softball team.
Fedora selects the kid who custom-coded the school website.

We could keep going, but that's probably all the information you need. If you were placing bets (which we know you never do), you'd probably know which team to pick. One of these teams wins before the game starts.

If you want to win a high school dodgeball game, you've got to stack your team with the right strengths. But if you want to win at small groups, you need to stack your team with small group leaders who have the right potential.

So, what makes a great small group leader?
It's simple.

They've got to follow Jesus.
They've got to like kids.
They've got to pass their background check.

Okay. That's an oversimplification. But really . . .

They don't have to be exceptionally gifted, but it helps if they're generous. They don't have to know everything, but it helps if they know what they don't know. They don't even have to be cool, but it helps if they can keep theirs.

When I (Kristen) was in high school, there was one leader who stood out from the rest. His name was Ralph, and when I think of him, I remember a thinly haired, scrawny man with a mustache and jean shorts. He stood out not only because he was absolutely the least trendy man in the room, but also because he literally stood outside our youth group. (It was called Power Source if you want to know.) He stood by the door as we came in, and he welcomed us. When he saw someone new, he talked to them. When a kid wanted to sit outside and smoke, he sat with them. (I'm sure some people questioned Ralph's judgment in the teenagers he allowed himself to hang around.) But Ralph formed the most unlikely connections. Students who might not have ever come back to church a second or third time came back because he was there and because they knew he cared about them.

There's one thing everyone has that has the potential of making him or her a great small group leader: A story. Their talent and gifting, the experiences and choices that have made him or her who they are, all make up a unique person with wisdom and insight to share. And as unique as people seem to be, there are others out there a few years younger whose story is very similar, just shorter. The power of leveraging that story for the benefit of the next generation is in everyone.

The point is this: Don't be too quick to disqualify someone from leading.

Anyone can be a great SGL.
But not everyone *should* be an SGL.

This idea isn't revolutionary. Your church probably already does this in other areas of ministry.

Think about it:

If you can't sing, you shouldn't be handed a mic.
If you don't know how to set up a Twitter account, you shouldn't be in charge of the church's social media presence.
If you're awkwardly shy, you should definitely not be on the greeter team.
And if you cry over weird smells, you probably shouldn't work with babies—or middle school boys.

We aren't saying some people shouldn't serve—everyone can serve somewhere. It's just that not everyone is meant to be an SGL. Your small group leaders are critical volunteers, and you can't afford to have leaders who aren't equipped or committed to the job. There's too much at stake.

If you're going to win before you begin, you've got to control the quality of the leaders on your team.

So now that you know what it takes to be a great small group leader, you may be wondering, "Do they offer them on Amazon Prime?"

Sadly they do not. And it takes longer than two days to get them.

In fact, with all of the traditions and denominations that have divided the Church, the one unifying experience that's shared around the world is that no one has enough small group leaders. Ever. Or if they do, they won't for long. But remember, things of great value are worth the effort it takes to get them. And there's nothing more valuable in ministry than a great small group leader.

The reality is, you'll never be done recruiting SGLs. So since this will be an ongoing part of your job until you become famous or move to the beaches of Caicos, we want to give you a few recruiting principles. Unlike dodge ball, the success of your ministry isn't connected to physical strength and agility. It's connected to how well you recruit, screen, and prepare your SGLs before they begin to lead. If you want to get in the habit of winning before you begin, there are a few things you should do.

You win before you begin when . . .
YOUR BEST LEADERS RECRUIT YOUR BEST LEADERS.

One year when I (Reggie) was leading our family ministry team at North Point, our preschool environment was in need of SGLs. Okay—that happened every year. But this particular year, early in our ministry, our pastor Andy Stanley asked for leaders from the platform. If you've ever heard Andy ask for volunteers, you know he can be pretty compelling. In a single day, after just one message, we had over 300 leaders signed up to serve preschoolers. It's good news for you that we aren't advocating this as your model, because I'm not sure anyone else can get that kind of result after one message.

We were happy with the results. We had more than enough leaders, so I assumed our recruitment troubles were over. At the end of the year, however, when it came time to reassign groups, only three of those 300 leaders remained. When I asked the

Groups Directors what was different about the leaders who stayed, they told me, "Those leaders are a different kind of leader. They recruited their friends to serve with them, and they feel more ownership in their role." So, I responded by asking our preschool team to go find 20 more leaders like those leaders. Instead of recruiting 300, it may be important to start by recruiting the right 20. If you recruit the right few, they'll help you recruit and keep the rest.

When we started North Point, we had few relationships or connections to potential volunteers. So, we began asking our existing SGLs to help us recruit new SGLs. At meetings, we handed out index cards and asked our SGLs to write down the names of two or three friends who could do what our SGLs were doing. Then we challenged them to recruit at least one of those friends to join them. We were amazed at the number of new volunteers our existing volunteers recruited when we leveraged their personal network.

When you want to find and attract the best leaders, casting a wide net isn't always helpful. An announcement from the platform or in a bulletin might draw a crowd, but in the long run, the time you'll spend sorting through any number of applicants can be more work than it's worth. When you inspire volunteers to join you in the recruitment process, however, you can cast your net to a more targeted group of people. You demonstrate trust in your SGLs when you ask for their input, and you make recruiting a team effort. And because your SGLs know what they're doing matters, and know what it takes to be a great leader, they can help you recruit leaders who will have longevity. Because, chances are, your best leaders will respond to a personal invitation, not an announcement.

Adam Duckworth is the Volunteer Coordinator at Downtown Harbor Church in Fort Lauderdale, Florida. He told us, "We recruit most of our SGLs by one-on-one recruiting—mainly by leaders recruiting other leaders. When our leaders see the value of their position, their passion overflows."

It will take work and time, but you can cultivate leaders who recruit other leaders. How? Find your best SGLs and have this conversation: "We need more people like you. Who do you know?"

You win before you begin when . . .
RECRUITING LEADERS IS A PROCESS, NOT AN EVENT.

Wouldn't it be great if recruiting small group leaders was as simple as an event? Imagine how fantastic it would be if we could write "Recruitment Day!" on our calendars, knowing this one day would yield all the SGLs we'd need for the entire year. What if we could simply list the number of SGLs we needed and stand back while a mob of enthusiastic, perfectly qualified people rushed to sign up? What if we could rest our heads on our pillows at night knowing we wouldn't even have to think about recruiting for another 365 days because—of course—our perfect new SGLs would never quit, move away, or do anything that would force us to fire them?

If you aren't sighing with longing right now—even a little bit—you probably didn't read that last paragraph very closely.

Big leader recruitment events can produce a lot of excitement and potentially a lot of warm bodies. But high-quality small group leaders are *cultivated* not *captured*. Cultivation requires a multi-step, 365-days-a-year process. If this sounds like a lot of work, it is. But the most important volunteer role in your church is worth the effort.

We work with hundreds of churches around the country, and while there are subtle differences in their processes, they all have a version of the following six steps.

1. INVITATION

"Could I have your attention please? Could I have your attention please? Would anyone be interested in filling a predetermined slot in our somewhat confusing organizational structure? If so, please go to room 204. Thank you."

Does your volunteer recruitment strategy ever feel a little like that? Here's the thing:

Volunteers respond to an announcement.
Leaders respond to an *invitation*.

Invite them into a life-changing opportunity that's bigger than they can imagine. The more personal the invitation, the better. Remember, the best invitation comes from a leader already serving.

Resist the temptation to lower the bar because you think it makes for an easier "yes." Great leaders are drawn to big challenges with big rewards. Cast a compelling high-bar vision and you'll get the great leaders you need.

2. ORIENTATION

"Why am I here? What am I supposed to do?" These are questions that every kid in your ministry will wonder about while they're with you.

These are *not* questions you want your SGLs wondering about. Great leaders want to know what their roles are and how they fit into the big picture.

That's the role of an orientation. Orientations are designed to turn interest into engagement. Inspiration, then information, is the target.

Some churches use one-on-one orientations, others do an event. Either way an orientation should . . .
Recast a compelling vision of why they're needed.
Familiarize them with the environment they'll be working in.
Clearly tie the expectations and commitments to the vision.
Do it all in such a way that you can wait on them to make the next move.

3. APPLICATION AND BACKGROUND CHECK

At this point, if the invitation and orientation have done their job (and by that we mean if you have done your job with them), then the purpose of the application and background check is to protect you—not to convince them. The leaders who are still there are convinced. You want leaders who want to be there.

Review the application and references carefully and *never* skip on the background check.

Pay attention to any red flags. No leader, no matter how badly you need one, is worth the pain and difficulties a bad leader can bring. You're far better off having a conversation now then dozens of conversations later. For yellow flags, make a note and include the questions in your interview.

4. INTERVIEW

The interview is the TSA of the recruiting process. It's the last thing standing between the potential leader and joining the team. So, this is serious business. This is your chance to ask any questions that arose in the application and to address any concerns you might have. Here are three things to consider when conducting an interview:

Hear from Them

Ask the leader to tell you their story. Why do they want to be an SGL? As you listen to their story, make sure they've caught the vision and listen for details that can help you when placing them. This is also the point when you ask for a verbal commitment to the requirements of the role. Sure, they should already be there by now, but there's nothing like having to verbally agree to solidify a commitment.

Let Them Hear from You

Everyone likes to work with their friends, so take this chance to make a friend. Tell them your story and why you love what you do. Remember, a personal vision is very compelling, and they wouldn't be here if they weren't looking for one of their own. As intense as that sounds, have fun. This should feel more like coffee with a friend than a job interview.

Consider Their Placement

This is the best time to begin considering the leader's placement. It could be based on need, but it should also be based on fit. You might need freshman leaders, but if a leader's story fits better somewhere else, look for a way to make it work. The more effective they are, the better the chance you have of retaining a leader year after year.

5.TRAINING

Some people mistakenly believe that the stronger the leader, the less training they'll want or need. Great leaders want to do a great job and understand that training is essential. Obviously this won't be their last training, but it will set the tone for all future trainings. If you set them up to succeed by giving them valuable information, they'll be there for every subsequent training. This is your opportunity to flesh out the mission, vision, and values of their role. Getting by on the nitty-gritty details will go a long way in securing a lasting commitment.

You might want to consider getting your leaders to sign a commitment stating that they've read and understand the policies and expectations you've laid out for them. Establishing this up front makes it easier to have future conversations about breaches in policies or expectations.

6. APPRENTICESHIP

Throwing a new swimmer into the deep end of the pool may work in some cases, but not when it comes to leading kids. Apprenticing is the key to making the transition from "willing candidate" to "great leader." It's so important, we'll talk more about it in a minute.

For those of you who are "Type-A, get-it-done folks" there's probably a little voice inside you saying, "I can get those six steps done in two, three weeks tops." And maybe you can, but if you want a sustainable ministry, you need to accept that recruitment will be an all-year process, not a once-a-year event.

The better your leaders, the more your ministry is going to grow. Which means you'll need more great leaders which means . . . you get the picture.

But leaders also move away or worse are "stolen away by those folks in that other ministry." (I know that never happens in your church, so this is for everyone else.) Whether you need more volunteers, or need to replace some spots, you can never *stop* recruiting.

Before you start feeling disheartened by this sentiment, remember this: you never know when an amazing SGL is going to show up. If your process is all built around one season of the year, you may have to ask a great candidate to wait (which means they may leave) or worse, lead when they haven't been vetted or trained (which means you may wish they had left).

Amy Fenton from The People's Church told us that, "We recruit through vision-casting in our adult service, emails, blog posts . . . any and every way possible to keep the mission and vision out there."

Bobbi Miller said that at her church in Texas, they created short-term service opportunities. "We'd recruit leaders to serve for just a day (like on Christmas or Easter), or for a few months in the summer. If we see someone who impresses us, we invite them to continue serving with us after their short-term commitment runs out."

You win before you begin when . . .
LEADERS PRACTICE LEADING BEFORE THEY LEAD.

Great leaders understand the value of a mentor or role model. It may seem a little odd to ask a new volunteer who works as a Corporate Executive to apprentice with a leader who might be younger and less experienced work-wise, but a great leader will welcome the chance to learn.

Allow your new SGL to co-lead for a while with one of your best, rock star leaders. By allowing them to observe someone you trust, you'll cement in them the vision of a great leader. This is the most critical step there is to reproducing leaders who do the job well. It will also go a long way in keeping the seasoned leaders, who you ask to be a mentor, engaged for the long term. One of the best things you can do to set your veteran leaders up for success is to make it clear to the new leader that they'll be getting feedback. Feedback not only from their mentor, but from their coach, and potentially you as well. If someone is expecting feedback, it can be received more easily than when it comes out of the blue.

Prospective SGLs are more successful when they make a solid connection with someone who can coach, encourage, and challenge them. Otherwise, the prospective leader might develop their own approach to leading a group that may not be consistent with your vision.

How does a veteran leader apprentice a new SGL?

Lead and let them watch you.
Let them lead with you.
Let them lead while you watch.

There are far more efficient ways of developing leaders than through apprenticing, but none are more effective. With SGLs, too much hangs in the balance to take shortcuts.

You win before you begin when . . .
YOU CREATE A PLACE WHERE LEADERS WANT TO BE.

If you Google the term "raving fan," you'll find dozens of strategies for how to create them. Ken Blanchard coined the term, but in many ways Chick-fil-A perfected the process. Creating raving fans means you've built a place that everyone can't stop talking positively about. Lots of people can create a place people talk about—it's the positivity part that's the key.

You want your leaders to be raving fans of your ministry. You want them to speak so positively about their experience that every potential leader they know wants to be a part of your team. So how do you do that? Well, what kind of culture do you like to be a part of?

Consider these questions:
Do your leaders *love* to come to your environment?
Do they have relationships with you and with each other?
Do they feel prepared, trained, and supported?
Do they feel valued and heard?

Everyone likes a place where they not only feel, but are communicated their value. Celebrate them. Give them "insider" information. Give them doughnuts, t-shirts, wristbands, fanny packs, or whatever you can think of that will help your leaders understand just how much you value them.

Creating an excellent culture also means making hard decisions. Despite your best efforts to find and recruit great leaders, you may still find yourself with someone who doesn't need to be an SGL in your ministry. Sometimes you have to protect the integrity of your culture by transitioning an SGL to a different role. If you don't let go of the wrong leaders, you might not attract the right leaders.

You may have many reasons for asking an SGL to transition to another volunteer position. Here are four:

An SGL can't meet the expectations of their role.
An SGL can't connect with an age group.
An SGL can't align with the direction of the ministry.
An SGL can't live the way they want to lead kids to live.

In any of those situations, it may be time for an SGL to transition to a different volunteer position. Transitioning an SGL will never be easy. But the more clearly and frequently you communicate your expectations to leaders up front, the easier these conversations will be when they happen.

Remember, your SGLs are some of your most significant volunteers. They're the "someone" you're intentionally placing in the life of a kid or teenager to shape their faith.

When you make it a habit to win before you begin, you recruit better leaders who will recruit better leaders.

CREATE EXPERIENCES
TO MAKE
RELATIONSHIPS MATTER.

That's because the impact of your message is amplified in the context of personal relationships.

Picture this. You run into the grocery store for some Double Stuf Oreos because you're out, and you really can't go another day without Double Stuf Oreos. You get to the checkout line. You're checking Twitter on your phone and scanning the tabloids to see if there are any great stories you can incorporate into this week's message. Then, as you scan your credit card, the cashier casually asks you, "On a scale of one to ten, how do you feel like your prayer life is going?"

No?

Okay, try this one. You're at the gym working out—maybe for the first time in a few months. The guy next to you is doing an intense routine, so you step aside to give him a little more room. He looks over at you, takes his earbuds out, smiles and says, *"The prudent see danger and take refuge, but the simple keep going and pay the penalty."*[6]

A little creepy?

If you don't think so, this next point may escape you. But for the rest of you, those who would be tempted to order a workout video that can be safely done inside your own home far away from smiley gym man, consider this: There are some things we earn the right to say in someone's life.

Maybe that's why when it comes to discipling the next generation, it's probably not a good idea to share your ideas about the Apocalypse before you know a kid's last name. Or why you might want to save your insights on moral purity until after you know the names of their parents. Or why you might not want to explain the benevolence of a loving Father before you know what happened in their world last week.

It's not that those truths aren't important.
It's not even that those truths can't be shared by a communicator on a platform.
It's just that some truths are better processed in the context of a relationship.

You'll always be able to communicate truth more effectively when you're communicating that truth through someone who has an ongoing, weekly relationship with a kid or teenager.

---

6. Proverbs 22:3, NIV

As church leaders, we feel tremendous responsibility to communicate the greatest message on the planet. We're driven by the mission to help every kid and every teenager understand they're loved by their Creator. We want them to understand that He sent His Son to die for them to give them a full life, both now and for eternity. We also believe by helping kids understand God's story of redemption and Biblical principles of wisdom, we can help them have a better future.

So, we care about the message. A lot. But if we care about the message in a way that makes us lose sight of who we're trying to impact, we may start to behave a little like that crazy guy at the gym.

But you're not a crazy guy at the gym. You believe the impact of your message has greater potential when it's communicated in the context of consistent, personal relationships.

Because you believe the impact of your message can be amplified by the context of personal relationships, you should create experiences every week to enhance small group connection.

Building a ministry where small group is the answer for discipleship means more than just organizing your ministry to connect kids in consistent groups with consistent leaders. It means more than recruiting and training SGLs who understand their role. It also means you'll be intentional about the way you create a weekly experience.

Before you get too excited about rethinking your weekly experience, let's be clear. We aren't going to suggest you disciple preschoolers with a weekly adventure to Chuck E. Cheese or that you help a kid trust in Jesus by taking them out to the park to play kickball or that the best plan to encourage a teenager to own their own faith is by organized laser tag.

Those things are all great. And you'll want to plan for some of that in the context of your calendar year if you want to help foster strategic relationships. But more than that, you *should* plan a weekly experience where kids can worship, hear Biblical truth presented in a relevant and direct way, and process that experience in small group. A small group culture doesn't mean you get rid of weekly programming. It simply means you change the way you prepare and evaluate your weekly experience when you understand the goal is always what happens in small group.

We've already said . . .
the primary place you want a kid to be is small group.
your answer for discipleship is small group.
your most important volunteer is the small group leader.

As you plan your weekly experience, you'll begin with the small group in mind. The problem is, when all is said and done, you can't control what happens in a small group. You can't force relationships to work. You can't make relational ministry predictable or perfect.

When your success is predicated on a relational connection, it can be tricky to plan and even harder to evaluate. But that doesn't mean it's impossible. Sure, there's a level of it that's out of your control. If you're a fan of a good calendar and a spreadsheet, if you like a weekly to-do list, and you rest better at night knowing it was a productive day, don't worry. There are still some things you can control, and it's actually a lot more productive to focus on those.

You can't make a kid talk during group,
but you can create a message that's
likely to provoke a conversation.

You can't make kids connect with each other,
but you can prepare content that will be
interactive, fun, and relevant.

You can't make leaders relate to their few,
but you can give them resources to set them up for success.

You can't create perfect small groups,
but you can do something every week to create experiences.

HAVE IMAGINARY CONVERSATIONS
(Let's talk about your content.)

I (Kristen) remember very clearly the day I discovered the value of imaginary conversations. I wasn't playing Strawberry Shortcake as a child, or grounded and bored. I was leading a small group of eleventh grade girls.

That night in small group, I asked a question that was followed by silence. No problem. As a fairly veteran leader, I was comfortable with the silence. I let it sit . . . and sit . . . and sit. And then I began to realize this wasn't the kind of silence where they were processing their answers. Instead, they were exchanging confused looks and uncomfortably averting their eyes. Then one savvy, sarcastic girl spoke up. "So, Kristen, can *you* answer that question?" Immediately all eyes were on me. Now it was my turn to be uncomfortably silent. No. I could not answer the question. It was a weird question. I just hadn't noticed until I put myself into my girls' place—or rather, they put me in it—and I had to respond.

After that day, I never asked a small group question again without reading through the list first. (Okay, that's not true. Some weeks are just busy.) But now I make every effort to have an imaginary small group conversation before I have an actual one. It changes what I will say in the room.

If you've ever . . .
sat through an interview,
broken up with a boyfriend,
called home with bad news,
proposed to a girlfriend,
or confronted a friend,
you've probably had an imaginary conversation.

You wanted a little bit of rehearsal time. You know that what you say in the moment can be said better if you anticipate what you're going to say (or not say).

As a church leader, you'll also need to have some imaginary conversations if you want to create a message that can be experienced in small group.

Remember, you have the greatest message of all time. But if you're lucky, you'll get forty hours this next year to tell a kid everything they need to know about God. That's not a lot. When you factor in sports, holidays, shared custody, you'll probably have far less time with your average attender to communicate everything you need to communicate.

That's a lot of pressure.

So, I'm going to say something that might sound a little harsh, but here it is: You're irresponsible if you aren't strategically planning your message. Yes, you'll have opportunities to influence kids and teenagers outside of your programming. But your weekly programming is the environment where you have their attention (at varying levels) for somewhere around an hour. So you should do everything you can do to make the most of that hour.

You need a comprehensive plan.
You need a clear bottom line.
You need relevant examples.
You need visual illustrations.
You need funny jokes.
You need practical applications.

Now, if you're starting to shut down and have some imaginary conversations with us about how some of the expectations in this book are just a little unrealistic, let us step in and respond. We aren't trying to paint an impossible picture. If you're working to improve your structure so you can support relational connection, and you're recruiting, training, and leading exceptional leaders who can be present in the lives of a few on a weekly basis, then you're a very busy person. We get that. That's why we think you shouldn't create your own curriculum. You should use a pre-designed curriculum and customize it.

> **You know that what you say in the moment can be said better if you anticipate what you're going to say (or not say).**

Okay, fair disclaimer: those of us who are writing this book also create curriculum. So, maybe you think it's self-serving for us to say you ought to use one. But let's put this in perspective for a minute:

You have around 40 work hours this week,
which means you'll probably spend . . .

15 hours in meetings with staff and SGLs,
10 hours answering email,
½ **hour** testing the fog machine so it doesn't set off the fire alarm,
1 hour disabling the fire alarm,
5 hours in conversations with parents and kids,
½ **hour** meeting about the next meeting,
10 hours setting up for, working, and cleaning up after
   programming,
1 hour making one more run to Costco for Goldfish Crackers and
   Dixie cups.

That leaves about **-3 hours** to think about your message this week.

And let's not begin to think about what the average week looks like
for part-time staffers and volunteers leading the ministry.

On our team, we have a team of full-time staff who work
directly to plan, write, script, act, edit, and produce monthly
curriculum . . . for one age-group. That's over **two thousand
people-hours** invested in every month for creating a strategic,
relevant, engaging message.

We do what we can do with our experiences and creative abilities
so you can do what only you can do: connect on the frontlines with
leaders and kids.

If I were your lead pastor, this is what I'd tell you, "I don't want
you to write your own curriculum. I need you to develop leaders
who love kids. I know you think you can do both. But you
can't. Even if you think you can write it a little better than an
organization that spends hundreds of thousands of dollars to write
it, the cost to your team and our church will not be worth the
difference. I'd rather you use a curriculum that you don't think is

as good as what you can do so you can leverage most of your time and budget to develop better leaders. Great volunteers are much more important than incrementally improving your curriculum." I understand that some of you have an itch to create what's taught every week. You can accomplish just as much and more if you tweak a curriculum that has editable documents.

If you still have a drive to be a writer or producer, do one or two great series each year, or submit a writing sample to one of the above organizations and join their creative team. A curriculum is worth whatever price you need to pay because it gives you more margin to invest in leaders.

Whether you use our curriculum or someone else's, it just makes sense to let someone give you a starting place. If you're in a unique situation where your role requires you to write your own curriculum, maybe you should appeal to leadership for some creative ways to find a curriculum partner. Then you can use the hours in your week to contextualize, customize, and personalize that message for your church.

You can use your imaginary conversations to bring someone else's words to life, to make them better, and to help them connect with those you're called to reach.

Have imaginary conversations so . . .
WHAT HAPPENS ON THE PLATFORM WILL PROMPT
WHAT HAPPENS IN THE SMALL GROUP.

Some things are communicated better from a platform than in a circle. That's why we think it's so important to structure your ministry in a way where large group environments work as a step to group, as a step to a better experience in group, and as a step to create a culture of groups. But there's also a relational benefit to letting a skilled communicator teach, so your small group leaders don't have to.

Putting the most dynamic, articulate teacher you have on the platform will inevitably improve your small group experiences. But you can take it a step further. Your communicators can leverage their message to prompt what happens in small group. And here are four practical ways to do that:

1. **START WITH THE SMALL GROUP EXPERIENCE.**
   Before you write a talk or customize a message, think about what you want to happen in group. Have an imaginary small group conversation. What do you hope they'll talk about? When you begin with the end in mind, it will change the way you set up the conversation.

2. **SAY WHAT YOU CAN SAY, SO THEY DON'T HAVE TO SAY IT.**
   Your SGL's primary goal is to give a kid a safe place to process faith. So when you leverage a master communicator to present truth, you do something remarkable for the group. You give them a leader who is neutral, someone who didn't just teach them something they may want to challenge. As you consider the message, think through what a master communicator can say from the platform so the leader can spend less time wearing a teacher hat, and more time facilitating the conversation.

3. **SET UP THE TENSION.**
   When a communicator explains the idea too thoroughly, answers every possible critique, and makes every possible application, there's very little left to talk about in small group. It seems counterintuitive for most communicators, but it helps the group experience when a communicator can leave a few things unresolved. It's okay to resolve tension when

you're communicating to preschoolers, but as kids get older, unresolved tension will become an important tool to keep kids engaged and to set up groups to win.

4. SAY ONE THING.

There's a limit to what a kid (or adult) can really process in one hour. Small group experiences help kids personalize and apply Biblical truth, but that can't happen when they have to spend the first half of group trying to figure out what the message was about. Your message should have one, clear bottom line. The clearer the message, the faster your small groups can get to application.

Have imaginary conversations so . . .
WHAT YOU SAY TO LEADERS DURING THE WEEK WILL GUIDE WHAT THEY SAY TO KIDS DURING SMALL GROUP.

Every leader wants a plan and a script for their group time. Without a script, your leaders might do nothing but talk about the mating habits of wild boar every week, or try to take their third-grade girls through *Mere Christianity*. Being relevant and strategic about your environments means you don't let your leaders run rogue. Instead, you spend a considerable amount of your week evaluating your small group materials.

If you want the application of your message to be experienced in a small group context, then the activities and questions you give your leaders are one of the most critical elements of your weekly curriculum. Effective activities and questions take time and *a lot* of imaginary conversations. Here are just a few things you should keep in mind.

1. ACCOMMODATE A VARIETY OF LEARNING STYLES.

Not every kid processes information in the same way. Some kids learn better by listening, some by talking. Some learn better by watching, some by doing. Since one style won't fit all, your activities should never be weighted too much toward one learning style.

2. CONSIDER THE AGE OF YOUR AUDIENCE.

A preschooler is very different than a first grader, and the mind of a first grader isn't the same as the mind of a third grader. When you evaluate your curriculum, the activities and questions should change according to the age and stage of the child. If child development isn't your thing, find an educator you trust, someone who understands child development, and have them review your small group curriculum. We actually wrote a whole book about this called It's *Just a Phase* to help church leaders understand how they can leverage the unique opportunities of each stage of a kid's life in their development of faith.

3. RELATE TO THE CULTURE OF YOUR DEMOGRAPHIC.

No curriculum will ever be exactly what you need for your context. So, take the material through some filters. Are the examples and applications reflective of your socioeconomic, ethnic, and regional make-up? How can you customize this material to leverage your particular culture for the sake of your message?

4. RARELY GIVE THEM SOMETHING THAT CAN BE ANSWERED WITH ONE WORD.

Whether the answer is "Yes," "No," "Jesus," or "The Bible," posing a question that can be answered with one word is typically a conversation killer. The exception to the one-word answer rule is if the question can be answered with a variety of singular words. "What's your favorite Olympic sport?" is a one-word question that can open a conversation.

5. DON'T CONFUSE A CONVERSATION GUIDE WITH A STUDY GUIDE.

The purpose of small group is to help kids process and apply biblical truth, not to help kids pass a biblical literacy test. That means your small group materials guide conversations. A study guide in an open group setting can quickly alienate kids who are less adept learners. If every question has a right answer, kids will determine for themselves whether they're smart enough or *not* smart enough to belong in church. Please don't miss this: Church isn't a place where smart people belong. It's a place where everyone belongs.

6. ASK SOME QUESTIONS "JUST FOR FUN."

Seriously.

Groups should be fun. If you want kids to come back, and if you want them to enjoy being with their leaders and with each other, then they probably need to laugh together. If they don't laugh together, they'll probably never feel comfortable enough to talk with each other about their questions, their doubts, or their life experiences. So, give them something fun to do and something fun to talk about—every week.

Have imaginary conversations so . . .

WHAT LEADERS THINK ABOUT *BEFORE* GROUP WILL AFFECT HOW THEY NAVIGATE THE CONVERSATION *DURING* GROUP.

As much time as you spend customizing a guide for your small group leaders this week (and you should), just realize your leaders may not stick to it (and they shouldn't). If you're empowering great leaders, they'll know their few better than you do. Which means they'll ultimately be the ones who have the imaginary conversations to contextualize specifically for their particular group.

Just remember, you have an advantage over your SGLs. You're in this full-time, or part-time, so you see the big picture. You understand the scope and cycle of your content. You know where you're headed and why. That's helpful information for the leader who will be navigating conversations in group next week. Every week, you should use every method of communication possible to help your leaders see the big picture. Send them a video. Send them a podcast. Send them a paragraph. Email them personally. Post something to a private leader group. Send them a short text. If you want to help them navigate their group time effectively, you have to help them think about a few things before they get there.

You can help your leaders navigate their group time when you:

1. TRAIN THEM TO MOVE AWAY FROM THE SCRIPT.

No leader guide is perfect. There are days when the activities flop, when the topic isn't connecting, or when the night before was Halloween and everyone has a sugar hangover. It happens. Let your leaders know they have your permission to do what they need to do—even if it means going a little off-script.

One day during small group time at Bobbi Miller's church, Bent Tree Bible Fellowship, she saw one of her leaders doing jumping jacks with his group of third graders in the hallway. This was *not* a part of the specified curriculum activities for the day. But they were jumping and saying the words to their memory verse. She told us, "The leader looked 'caught' and apologized as he explained to me that his group always has a lot of extra energy and he was trying to find ways to engage them. I told him it was brilliant! I was so glad he felt the freedom to improvise, letting those boys put their energy to work."

Matt Ivy has been a small group leader for student groups for over 10 years, and told us that whenever his group gets stuck or the questions just aren't working, he asks one question: "Who would win in a fight: a bear or a gorilla?" And their group would resume their ongoing debate. "It might not have given a lot of spiritual insight, but for my tenth-grade guys it let them connect and kept our group fun instead of letting things get awkward."

2. GIVE THEM A CLEAR DESTINATION.

If your leaders are going to go off-script, they need to know where they're headed. When you're in week one of a series, let them know the bottom lines for week two and three so they won't accidently cover next week's idea this week and regret it later. Give them a clear goal for their conversation this week so that even if they don't follow the plan and the script, they know what a win looks like.

3. ALERT THEM TO FORESEEABLE CHALLENGES.

When you're covering a story about Lazarus with kindergartners, kids may have questions about death. When you talk about miracles with third graders, they may ask you about their sick grandmother. When you talk about respect for authority with students, there may be some who present some challenging scenarios. If you're covering a topic that's likely to raise some challenging questions, give your leaders a heads up. It's always easier to navigate when you aren't caught off-guard.

When you get in the habit of having imaginary conversations before group, you cooperate with what's already happening so groups happen better.

158

CONTROL THE CLIMATE
(Let's talk about your context.)

O kay, no one can really control the climate. And no
ministry leader can fully control the experience every
kid has in small group. But there are external factors you
can control as a staff member that affect the quality of the group
experience. These are the factors that make up your physical space.

As you create a culture in your ministry where every kid has a
place to belong, don't make the mistake of under-thinking your
physical space. Relationships may be what connect them to your
ministry, but what you do with your physical spaces can support
those relational connections or undermine them.

If you don't believe me, think about . . .
American Girl
Legoland
Starbucks
Disney

A few years ago, I (Kristen) had one of the most magical days of
my life. I say "magical" because at thirty-two years old, I finally
experienced my first day at the Magic Kingdom. Growing up I
never went to any Disney park, so this was literally the experience
of a lifetime. I paid one lady one time, and she handed me a
Mickey bracelet and a pin with confetti on it to celebrate my first
Disney experience. I never had to pay again. Any time I wanted
anything, I just bumped the Mickey bracelet and I had it—like
magic. When I entered the park and turned down Main Street
I was greeted by a parade of people dancing and singing and

celebrating me and my big day. When I met the Mouse himself, he spoke to me as if the living, breathing cartoon character had stepped out of the Big Screen just to welcome me. He even complimented my seven-year-old companion on her beautiful Elsa dress. We used a Fast Pass to avoid lines. We experienced cool mist blown onto us out of thin air when the day warmed up. The ambient music changed subtly as we moved from Tomorrowland to Adventureland to Fantasyland. I never saw a single piece of trash or anyone carrying out the trash.

What was unbelievably remarkable about my trip to Disney is this: I had waited for this day for thirty-two years, but they welcomed me when I arrived as if they had been anticipating my arrival with as much expectancy as I had.

We have a few friends who work for Disney parks, and in spite of what it felt like to experience the park, I know what I experienced wasn't actually magic. It's the result of a lot of hard work and deliberation. With an average of 46,000 visitors per day, even Magic Kingdom has to be strategic about how to dispose of trash in a way that isn't intrusive—the fairy dust doesn't really just blow it all away.

Memories can be made in any environment, but there are some environments that foster connection in a better way because someone has taken the time to control the climate.

You may not be starting with the most attractive or practical physical space. You probably don't have the budget of Disney parks. The space may not even be your own if you're in a mobile or multi-purpose environment. But there are things you can control that will let every guest know you were thinking about them before they got there, and you care about the experience they have while they're with you.

Before we move into some of the characteristics of an environment that supports relational connections, it's important to make this one observation. You don't see your physical space the same way a first-time guest sees it. When you live somewhere for too long, when you work somewhere too often, there are things you stop noticing. They become part of the unseen backdrop of your life.

There were actually a few times I (Reggie) paid high school kids in our community to come sit in our weekly environment for teenagers. I wasn't trying to manipulate our numbers. I wanted to hear their perspective. What was the experience like for them? Was there anything about the experience that was off-putting or "weird"? We also know some leaders who church-swap by inviting a neighboring pastor to come to their environment—not to show it off, but to help each other see what the other no longer sees.

For the next few pages, we thought we'd identify a few characteristics of spaces that work when it comes to creating environments where every kid knows they belong.

Control the climate so . . .
YOUR PHYSICAL SPACE WELCOMES EVERYONE.

Sometimes I wonder what could happen in any environment if the people in charge began to act like today was their customer's first experience with them. My first visit to Disney wasn't the first time Mickey greeted a guest. It wasn't the first time the characters paraded down Main Street. And it wasn't the first time Cinderella talked to a raving adult fan. But they made it feel as if it were. They greeted us, welcomed us, and directed us so there was never an awkward or out-of-place moment.

If you want kids to know they belong when they're in group, make sure they feel like they belong before they get to group.

From the moment a kid or their parent drives onto your property, every guest should know where they're supposed to go. As soon as they enter your physical space, let them know you've been expecting them. If you have a parking lot, how are you welcoming them and showing them where to enter the building? If you live in a walking city, who stands at your door to greet them when they walk in? You can position volunteers to greet and welcome guests every step of the way. And you can control how those volunteers make a kid feel.

If they don't know where to go, they won't feel like they belong.

Control the climate so . . .
YOUR PHYSICAL SPACE APPEALS TO YOUR AUDIENCE.

When you invite guests to your home, what do you do? You clean up. You organize the clutter, you sweep the floor, you light a candle. If they're staying overnight, you change the sheets, lay out clean towels, and make sure to have food and drinks on hand. When you know someone is coming over, you let them know you were thinking about them before they got there.

If you're expecting guests to show up at your church, you should behave the same way. Maybe don't lay out clean towels, because that would be weird. But make your physical spaces appealing.

If hosting has never come naturally to you, here's a practical tip. Each week, have someone walk through your environments and play the sense game. Ask these questions:

What does it sound like?

What does it smell like?

What does it look like?

What does it feel like?

You might not be able to control some of the smells in your environments after they arrive, but you can start things off right—and you can keep a can of Lysol handy. The temperature, the lighting, the seating, and the décor all matter when it comes to making kids feel at ease in your church.

Small group environments can be challenging—especially when you're creating them in shared spaces. Just remember, what works for adults probably doesn't work for second graders. And what works for preschoolers won't translate well for high school juniors. If you've ever walked through Pottery Barn Kids or Pottery Barn Teen, it's obvious someone in that organization understands different ages. What's impressive is how they take a large, open store-front space and create sectioned-off, age-specific environments that let you feel as if you've stepped right into the world of a fourth-grade boy.

In the same way, when you create small group spaces for kids and teenagers, keep your target audience in mind. Whether you have a traditional church facility, a mobile set-up, a large auditorium, or a movie theater, section your spaces off to give them a place of their own.

"The best small group we ever had with kindergartners was when we met in the chapel. The pews and the stained glass made us all feel reverent and it kept us focused."—no small group leader ever.

Adam Duckworth, at his church in Fort Lauderdale, shared with us in his environments, "For preschoolers, we have tables and chairs for small groups because of the hands-on nature of some of the activities. But for kindergarten and first grade, we use carpet circles."

At Gina McClain's church in Tennessee, they used rugs to designate their group space. "Circle rugs have gone a long way toward defining the amount of space a group has and reminding them of the value of small. When a group decides to combine or keeps growing, it's a constant visual reminder that the group is too big."

I (Shef) believe in private meeting places for groups in middle school. They need to feel safe. It doesn't have to be a room, per se, but it needs to be a place where you don't have to worry about people listening. We actually converted our church offices to middle school small group rooms so it's a good stewardship of space.

Some ministries have high school groups that meet Sunday evening or mid-week in order to provide them with optimal spaces. Some ministries convert large rooms so they're more conducive to small group focus. Some ministries move their small groups off-site. The goal is all the same. Give them a place they can call their own. And give them a space that appeals specifically to them.

Control the climate so . . .
YOUR PHYSICAL SPACE COMMUNICATES YOUR MESSAGE.

When I (Kristen) was a high school teacher, one of my favorite things was rearranging my room. Maybe it's because any change is a good change when your room is four square walls of cinderblock with fluorescent lighting and concrete floors. But I simply loved setting the stage for what was going to happen. I wanted students to walk through the doors with an expectation that something could happen in the room that was more than what the classroom shell conveyed. On test days it was a classroom, but when we started a unit on suspense, the lights were off, electric candles were lit, and creepy music played on the boom box from the corner. (Yep. It had a tape deck.) When we studied *Lord of the Flies*, they walked in to the theme music for *Lost* and the desks were arranged by "island." When we had debate conversations, the desks were arranged in one large inner circle and one large outer circle.

No matter how simple or complex your physical space and no matter how mobile your environments, you can use your space to communicate your message.

Using your physical spaces to communicate your message doesn't mean your spaces have to be elaborate. In fact, sometimes a simpler physical space can work to your advantage. We have a friend who inherited a jungle. Literally. It was a fun-looking space, but the problem was they weren't talking about jungles every week, and over time the jungle began to compete with their weekly message. The context of your environment should complement the content, not distract.

In the same way, if your space stays the same for too long, whatever your messaging is, it will get lost. It can become white noise. But when you intentionally rearrange your space and change out elements of the design, your physical space can enhance the weekly message in a fresh, new way.

How does this apply to small groups? Think about all the ways you can customize your space so kids and teenagers can visually see what you want to communicate. What are you putting on your walls to help kids remember the bottom line? What are you putting in the hallways and throughout your physical spaces that will make your message stick?

Control the climate so . . .
YOUR PHYSICAL SPACE EQUIPS YOUR LEADERS.

If you've led ministry for over a week, you know this: your volunteers need resources to be successful. They need Bibles. They need activity supplies. They need conversation guides. But if you're creating a small group culture, you'll be especially concerned with how your environments provide the resources your small group leaders need.

As a children's director, Gina McClain talks about reorganizing the way she resources leaders so she can reinforce their belief in small groups. She transitioned from a system of "curriculum carts" (holding enough supplies for an entire grade level), to a cart holding individual tubs of supplies with just enough materials for each small group. Gina said, "It made a huge difference in how our SGLs viewed their group."

When your physical space equips your leaders, they're free to focus on their few. They know they can create an experience in their group because they trust they'll have whatever they need on hand to make that happen. When you use your space to resource your leaders, you control the climate and foster an environment where groups can win.

Control the climate so . . .
YOUR PHYSICAL SPACE IS SAFE.

Educational theorists have written about this for years—physical needs precede our ability to process emotionally and intellectually.

For some students, the only feeling of true safety may be in your halls. Their home context may leave them physically hungry and tired, making it difficult to focus on the group conversation. If you want small groups to work, the kids in your groups need to feel safe. So, make sure your physical spaces actually *are* safe. If they aren't safe, very little else will matter. You've probably already thought of this, which is why you probably have already done most of the things on this list. That's great! Consider it a list to show others how much you're already doing.

1. RUN BACKGROUND CHECKS.

Background checks aren't one-hundred-percent preventative, but they're an important guard to put in place to help your environment stay safe.

2. HAVE A CHECK-IN SYSTEM AND A BATHROOM POLICY.

Never leave a kid alone without an adult. Never leave a kid alone with only one adult. Have automated systems and policies to ensure every kid is accounted for.

3. COMMUNICATE YOUR POLICY ON USING PERSONAL FUNDS TO HELP KIDS.

You've recruited great people. And when they get connect with a kid who struggles with finding food to eat on a consistent basis, they'll want to step in and help. Your church may already have a policy in place to help adults and kids in these situations, so make sure those policies are communicated to your SGLs so they know the best way they can help their few.

4. ELIMINATE THE OBVIOUS HAZARDS.

Kids will get hurt and kids will break stuff. Some things are inevitable, but every week you should run a basic safety check to avoid the dangers and liabilities that are avoidable. Are the outlets in your toddler spaces covered? Are the scissors in your elementary spaces put away? Have you removed the clay chalice your executive pastor brought back from the Holy Land from the table in your eighth-grade guys small group room?

5. CONTROL THE ENTRANCES, THE EXITS, AND THE ALLEYS.

We aren't saying you create environments as unassailable as Alcatraz. But while kids and teenagers are with you, you have a responsibility to make sure they don't leave and no one leaves with them. If you work with students, remember being seventeen. If you leave the pews unmonitored, someone will make out in them. And when Melissa's mom picks her up from your ministry with a hickey that wasn't there when she dropped her off, you will answer for it. Don't let Melissa get a hickey during student ministry. Monitor your hallways.

You don't have to create a bracelet with a chip in it to monitor the movements of every child, but you'd be surprised at what soap, paint, a piece of round carpet, and working air conditioning can actually do for your space. Controlling your environment may begin with some basics.

A few years ago, we went to a church in southern California with a student building that was separate from the rest of the church. Since it was in SoCal, the temperatures were fairly moderate, which is why the deacons of the church weren't overly concerned that the student space didn't have centralized air. The youth pastor put in a budget request several years in a row. After being continually denied, he did something creative. He scheduled space in the main building during the deacons' meeting and had the deacons meet in the student space in mid-July. The next year when he put in a request for AC, it was approved.

Whatever improvements you want to make in your physical spaces, begin with baby steps. You won't have the budget or the volunteer staff to get there overnight. So, start small. Make incremental changes. Control the climate every week so your physical space . . .

welcomes everyone.

appeals to your audience.

communicates the message.

equips your leaders.

is safe.

When you get in the habit of controlling the climate of your ministry, you'll create a context where what you say can actually be heard.

MEASURE WHAT SEEMS UNMEASURABLE
(Let's talk about your connections.)

S ome things in life are easy to measure.
How many times did you tweet?
How many Double Stuf Oreos did you eat?
How many miles per gallon does your vehicle get?

Some things in life are harder to measure.

How much water is in the ocean?
How many people live in Ukraine?
How much milk can a seventh grader drink without puking?

Then there are some things that seem unmeasurable.

How much does a mother love her child?
How do you know when someone is "over" their ex?
How well does a foster child integrate into a new home?

When it comes to the things that seem unmeasurable, you notice a common element: relational connections. People don't have high-tech digital monitors to indicate how connected they feel. There isn't a "mood ring" or a hyper-color t-shirt (remember those?) to let you know if every kid feels like your ministry is a place where they belong. Wouldn't it be great if there were?

Even though you can't visually, tangibly measure the depth of a relationship or the degree to which someone is connected, you can observe a few things that will indicate whether or not a kid feels known.

The most basic indicator is something pretty profound:
A kid will feel known when someone knows them.

Seriously. When there's a consistent leader who knows their name, their dog's name, and the way they like to fix their hot dog with relish and cheese and no mustard, then a kid will feel known. And there's a good chance kids need to feel known by someone before they'll feel known and loved by God.

Have you ever thought about the fact that there's a connection between *knowing* and *caring*?

Maybe that's why the psalmist wrote about God's intricate knowledge of creation.
> *He determines the number of the stars and calls them each by name. Great is our Lord and mighty in power; his understanding has no limit.*[7]

Or why there is an entire Psalm dedicated to God's knowledge of us.
> *You have searched me, LORD, and you know me.*
> *You know when I sit and when I rise; you perceive my thoughts from afar. You discern my going out and my lying down; you are familiar with all my ways. Before a word is on my tongue you, LORD, know it completely. You hem me in behind and before, and you lay your hand upon me.*[8]

---

7. Psalm 147:4-5, NIV
8. Psalm 139:1-5, NIV

Or why Luke reminds us that God knows the very number of hairs on our head.

That's a pretty strange thing to know when you really think about it. Why hairs on our head? It seems like a random thing to mention. But we think the purpose is simple: God wants us to know how much He knows, because it shows how much He cares.

If you want to measure the success of your weekly experiences, you should ask two questions.

Are kids connected?
Are they known?

That may seem like an over-simplification. But, remember you can't measure something until you've taken the time to define what really matters. When it comes to creating a culture of small groups, your goal is to give a kid a *person* and a *place* so they'll know they belong. So, your measurements should be designed to evaluate how well you're succeeding at that goal.

And you do need measurements.

Just like . . .
a poet knows words,
a mathematician knows formulas,
Shef knows physics,
you actually need to know some details about your ministry.

Knowing shows you care—and it may actually make you care more.

If you aren't wired for structure, it may not come naturally for you to focus on details and numbers and reporting. But there are some details that matter too much to be ignored, which is why someone in your ministry should know. Someone should own the weekly job of evaluating your ministry to see if connection is happening.

If you're still not big on trying to measure the unmeasurable, maybe this is something to consider. You might as well evaluate what you do. Chances are, someone else is already looking over your shoulder to gauge how well they think your ministry is working.

Maybe it's a senior or executive pastor.
Maybe it's the parents.
Maybe it's the kids or teenagers.

> **""**
>
> # A kid will feel known when someone knows them.

Here's a question. Who decides which yardsticks should be used to measure what you do? If you aren't a part of clarifying the win for your ministry, someone else will be. If you aren't proactively evaluating your ministry, others will evaluate it for you. And if someone is evaluating you by a different standard, you can imagine how well your ministry will measure up: kind of like NFL quarterback RG3 competing on *Iron Chef America*.

Don't let an outsider evaluate your ministry for you. Determine what the win looks like as a team, then proactively evaluate your weekly experiences. Let everyone agree on the standard you're using to measure success, then invite them to give you feedback.

Just remember: **There will still be times your ministry will feel unmeasurable. That's because you can't measure what's happening in the mind of a kid. You can't measure what's happening spiritually in their life. You can't measure what they're feeling emotionally.**

But there are some things every ministry can do to measure connection.

You measure the unmeasurable when you . . .
COUNT THE NUMBERS.

I know what you're thinking, *"This isn't about numbers."* Well, maybe in some ways it is. Numbers will never tell the whole story. But they'll always tell part of it if you know how to interpret them. You can't quantify spiritual growth. But you can look to the numbers as an indicator of some things. Maybe it helps to think of your ministry numbers like the scores in gymnastics.

When you're watching gymnastics on television and the judges flash what seems like an arbitrary number on the scoreboard, it's easy to think to yourself, *"That's subjective."* But the scores aren't arbitrary. They're guided by clear and consistent guidelines. Every skill has an optimum value, and every error made deducts from that total. Are the judges perfect? No. Will the score capture the essence of the performance? No. But the number the judges give for each routine will quantify something about the skill level and performance so it can be evaluated in comparison with another.

Remember, it's hard to manage what you can't measure. It's hard to improve your weekly experiences if you don't have a system of evaluation.

There are a few things you can measure quantitatively when it comes to your weekly experiences:
How often do kids come back?
Are they inviting friends?
Are new baptisms taking place?
Is your attendance up or down?

As you track these numbers, you are the interpreter of the data. Work with your team to interpret what they mean. If numbers are up, is there a reason you think it happened? If numbers are down, is there an explanation for why you think the drop is occurring? What do you know about the demographic of your community that informs your interpretation of data? Because if you lead a church in Chandler, Arizona, your numbers may be down in early March simply because it's hard to compete with the live ostrich race happening right outside your doors.

You measure the unmeasurable when you . . .
READ THE CROWD.

A skilled communicator on the platform can read the room. He or she can tell when the audience is leaning in, or when their attention is waning. As a communicator reads the room, they make adjustments to help their message connect with their audience. In the same way, you can read the connections in your ministry. But unlike a communicator, the information you need isn't sitting in front of you. You have to first identify who your audience is.

You have three crowds to read on a consistent basis:

KIDS OR STUDENTS

You're probably already reading the crowd when it comes to your most immediate audience. As you read them to see if they're connecting, you might ask yourself some of these questions:

Who do they talk about?

Who are they introducing their friends to?

Are they tweeting, posting, and talking about what happens in group?

The more you create a culture where kids belong in group, the more you'll hear them talk about their group experience. So, look for ways they're showing or not showing signs of that connection.

PARENTS

Parents are paying attention to what happens with their kid or teenager when they're with you. You probably don't need us to tell you that. You get their emails. But your parents aren't simply your raving fans or your harshest critics. They can be one of the greatest indicators of whether or not you're creating a culture where kids know they belong.

When it comes to parents, here are some questions to ask to help you read your audience:

> Do parents know the name and contact information of their kid's SGL?
>
> Do parents see the SGL as a partner? Do they connect with the SGL directly?
>
> What do parents celebrate about your ministry, and what frustrates them?

At Amy Fenton's church Tennessee, she says, "We're always listening to parents and their feedback. It's one of the keys to our ability to evaluate our ministry. They know when their kids aren't connecting. Sometimes it's an indication of a personality issue and we need to put a particular kid in a different group. Sometimes it's a red flag that life-change isn't happening in a group as a whole and something bigger needs to change."

SMALL GROUP LEADERS

If you're giving ministry away to leaders, you should be reading the leaders to see if connection is really happening. As you listen to the leaders, pay attention to what they're frustrated about. They *will* be frustrated. A successful small group culture won't mean you've eliminated the frustrations of all your leaders. It will mean you've shifted to a culture where your leaders are frustrated by the same things that frustrate you.

When you create a culture where every leader understands their role to connect with kids, they'll be

more frustrated by . . .

not having enough time to connect.
kids who can't find a ride.
noise that distracts when a kid wants to share a story.

less frustrated by . . .

a disruptive child who talks when they're talking.
games that take time away from the lesson.
not having enough chairs for the classroom.

Beyond their frustrations, listen to the stories they celebrate. What are they saying and what are they not saying?

Life is messy. When you create a system of relational ministry, you should expect some messy stuff. When kids have an adult who has given them a safe place, they're likely to share some things that will have you putting a licensed counselor on speed dial. If nothing messy is coming up, it may be an indicator that you still have a way to go to make the kids in your ministry feel like they have a safe place.

If you're unsure how to get this feedback from your SGLs, try something I (Shef) did. We held quarterly focus groups with a few select SGLs that we knew understood the vision of the ministry. We posed a few broad questions, and then let them talk. Not only did our staff learn how to handle certain issues from our volunteers, but the volunteers had a chance to learn from each other.

You measure the unmeasurable when you . . .
ASK KEY QUESTIONS.

If reading the crowd is how you observe the culture around you, asking questions is like taking the official census. There are some things you may not ever hear if you're simply being intentional about listening to what leaders are saying on their own—unprompted.

You need regularly scheduled times to ask your leaders some key questions.

Some questions are benchmarks.

You've asked your SGLs to take on a pretty significant role in a kid's life, so it only makes sense that you'd follow up with them to see how kids are connecting. If the success of your ministry is connected to their success in group, you should be asking things like:

Are the kids on your roster showing up?
Who has stopped coming?
Who are you having trouble connecting with?

It's not realistic for every leader to connect with every kid you put on their roster. But they may be your best resource for identifying anyone who is getting lost and coming up with a better plan to connect them.

Whatever expectations you've set out for your leaders, don't be afraid to ask them how it's going. Evaluating their success is a part of how you evaluate your success as a ministry.

Some questions prompt stories.

Some leaders share their stories unprompted, others may need for you to ask some questions to prompt their stories. So, when you connect with your leaders weekly to ask for specific feedback, remember to ask questions that will lead to stories. Questions like:

> What's the best thing that happened in your group lately?
> What do you have coming up in your group that you're excited about?

Some questions generate feedback.

As you evaluate your leaders, your leaders are evaluating you. They have insights about your ministry. So, when and where are you giving them an opportunity to share their thoughts with you? When you meet with your leaders weekly, ask questions to invite their input. Questions like:

> Do you have the resources you need for group time?
> Are you able to fill the time you have every week, or are you constantly running out of time?
> What's one thing that would help make your group experience better?

Then there's one more question you should ask every SGL every time you meet. It's pretty simple, but incredibly powerful.

How can I help?

Leaders need permission to ask for help when they need it. If you ask them regularly how you can help, you train them to know it's okay for them to come to you for assistance. Their answers to this question will help you know more about what's working and what's not working as you measure the experience that happens in groups.

When you meet with leaders to measure the unmeasurable, remind them that this is a long-term investment. You're on the same team. Collectively, you're thinking beyond today. There will be some weekly experiences that leaders and kids will talk about years later, and there will be some experiences that seem to make very little impact.

Sue Miller says, "Don't expect 'a moment' to happen every week. If they connected, that's a moment."

As important as measuring and improving your ministry is, you'll never measure everything in ministry. There will always be things happening that you can't see. And if you can't see it, you can't measure it. In 1 Corinthians, Paul explains an important principle about discipleship with a farming analogy. I'm not sure if you've ever grown anything, but it must have worked in that context.

*I planted the seed, Apollos watered it, but God has been
making it grow. So neither the one who plants nor the one
who waters is anything, but only God, who makes things
grow. The one who plants and the one who waters have one
purpose, and they will each be rewarded according to their
own labor. For we are co-workers in God's service; you are
God's field, God's building.*[9]

The successes of your ministry aren't yours alone. There are
others who have gone before you to love and influence the kids
and teenagers you serve. There will be others after you who will
continue to influence those who passed through the doors of
your ministry. Your ministry will produce results that you will
never see, but someone down the road may see them. That's why
you can't give up. You have to keep being faithful with the time
and influence you have. You measure what seems unmeasurable
because there's too much at stake. The job you've been called to do
matters.

And remember, it's "God who makes things grow"—not you. God is
at work in the lives of kids. You can plan and execute and measure
and improve, but you also need to trust. Trust that there's more
happening than what you can see, and more to your investment
than you can really measure. Trust that God is up to something
bigger and greater than you can imagine.

**When you get in the habit of measuring the unmeasurable,
you significantly increase your chances of making sure every
kid feels known.**

---

9. 1 Corinthians 3:6-9, NIV

Concert,
Classroom,
Circles

DO MORE THAN A CONCERT

Some of you are already implementing a small group strategy. We hope this book has reinforced much of what you already know and has given you some tangible ways to improve. Others of you are still in transition. You may be holding on to the positive things that have existed in your church's tradition, while at the same time trying to reinvent your ministry to be more relevant to the needs of a changing culture. (That's just another way of saying you're trying to change things without making someone mad.)

So, let's talk about change.

If you're going to transition something, it's important to know where you are and where you want to go. We have a friend who always says, "You're not transitioning if you don't know what you're transitioning to." That's why we think it's critical to discuss a few other basic approaches related to how some churches do children and student ministry.

We typically don't think labels are fair. Primarily, they're not fair because they tend to narrowly define a model or approach in a way that doesn't adequately represent all the facts. So, when we use a term to describe a model, it's not an attempt to attach a label, but to identify certain characteristics of one approach so we can clarify the potential differences in another approach. That being said, let's take a look at one model that has been traditionally used to minister to kids and teenagers.

The Concert Model

The concert model is focused on gathering the maximum number of kids in a room and making an engaging presentation. We use the word *concert* because of the similarity it has to a rock concert. It draws a crowd. It usually involves a level of production, is personality-driven, and has a band. The concert model for kids usually attempts to be a "more hip" version of what's happening in adult "big church." Many churches have traditionally built large rooms where they can do children's church and youth services, complete with age-appropriate music and teaching.

I (Reggie) was actually groomed as a student pastor in the concert model, along with a host of my friends in ministry. Some of us who started North Point even joke that one of the secrets to our growth is that we just kept doing student ministry for the adults who grew up. The concert model is an effective way to craft your skill as a speaker and to engage a crowd of people to worship corporately. If it's done strategically and with excellence, it provides a front door to engage people with core truths of the Christian faith and to connect people to the church. Through the years, I've been aware of thousands of kids and teenagers who were influenced to trust Christ and become engaged in ministry because of effective weekly gatherings like these.

The appeal of the concert model is that . . .
It's the fastest way to communicate to the most kids or students.
It only needs a limited amount of volunteers.
It's typically easy to measure and manage.

In a concert model, it's fairly obvious when things are working.
People . . .
laugh,
applaud,
talk back to you,
tweet what you say,
smile,
and in some cases, even go to an altar.
(Try explaining an altar to un-churched parents sometime.)

If teenagers enjoy it, they'll come back. Most children have to
come back whether they like it or not because their parents make
them. But when it comes to the concert model . . .
You can count the seats and know how many attend.
You can monitor the quality of the production.
You can usually know if it's working.

The primary limitation to the concert
model is when it ends, kids leave.
And at that point no one is really connected
to anything, except the experience.
The goal is to make that experience as engaging as
possible so kids will come back every week.

The other thing to realize about the concert model is that it
typically has a lot of competition outside the church. It's difficult
for churches to produce a quality experience that can measure up
to what's happening in culture.

You may have that deacon in your church
who knows how to juggle,
but Disney has Mickey.

You may have the teenager who almost made it through the first
round of *The Voice*, but next Sunday JT is doing a concert in town.

I've worked with churches that have invested thousands or hundreds of thousands of dollars in creating unique concert-type experiences. I've seen some pretty amazing productions designed for kids and teenagers. (We already wrote about why we think every church should do its best to create excellent environments.) But so far, I haven't seen any church consistently out-produce Disney, MTV, Nickelodeon, or put on a show like Barry Manilow—uh . . . I mean, Justin Timberlake. The sobering truth is that regardless of how much money your church spends, it will never really consistently compete with what most million-dollar entertainment entities can produce.

> **Although the average church can never compete with what culture can produce, culture can never compete with what the average church can do in the life of a kid.**

Please carefully consider this next point.
Although the average church can never compete
with what culture can produce,
*culture can never compete with what the average
church can do in the life of a kid.*

To state it another way, whenever the church gives kids a
safe place to belong with people who believe in them, it does

something nothing else in culture can do. Loving people unconditionally is a unique contribution the church can make. Regardless of your location, size, or budget, you are called, gifted, and empowered by the Holy Spirit to connect with and care for people. When you fulfill that calling, you're doing something no other entity can match. Why wouldn't you learn to play to your strength as a church? Recognize that while you may have limited resources and need to economize financially, it's vital not to economize the one area of your ministry with the most potential. Prioritize for relationships.

Another limitation of the concert model is the capacity of the personality on stage. We've talked a lot about capacity, but that's because we think it matters. It's critical to embrace the idea of building a healthy relational model around more than one personality. Ironically, the very personality at the center of making the concert model successful also has the potential to determine if a small group model is successful.

We were fortunate enough to work next to a lead pastor, Andy Stanley, who strategically managed the tension between the concert model and small groups. On one hand, our church recognized the giftedness of a unique communicator who could inspire thousands, and we built the right facilities to create a front door to welcome the community into our church. On the other hand, that same leader was committed to making small groups the priority. He built a team who was always quick to champion and fund a relational ministry to kids and teenagers.

We're not suggesting a concert model is wrong. We're boldly stating it's not enough.

If you have a ministry designed around a concert model, you need to consider making some adjustments. If you have a concert model that exists alone, without a clear, intentional strategy to move people into relationships, it can be dangerous. The concert should primarily exist to get people into circles where they can connect with others.

We have numerous conversations every week with churches that built their children or student ministries around a concert approach. Some of those churches are picking up the pieces of an unhealthy ministry because someone left, and all the fans of that individual followed or quit. Some are in a power struggle between a ministry leader who has built a platform and other leaders who are trying to refocus the ministry relationally.

When you're trying to transition to a relational model, you need to be aware of the potential tensions that can exist between concerts and circles.

Whenever a concert is the primary focus of a ministry . . .
it can make you feel like you're more or less
successful than you may actually be.
it can require so much energy or budget
that small groups can't win.
it can encourage stage personalities who
resist giving others influence.

So, if you want to be successful at implementing a culture where relationships matter . . .
you have to avoid letting concerts overshadow
what happens in your circles.
you have to groom leaders on stage to be more
interested in what happens in circles.
you have to allow your concerts to be influenced
by those in charge of circles.

Sure, concerts can be fun and exciting.
Concerts can be amazing experiences.

Concerts can be effective at inspiring a lot of people.

But just remember:
After the music stops,
and the emotion has faded,
and the lights are turned out,
and the doors have been closed,
it's what happens in a small group afterward that really lasts.

You will never disciple kids in a crowd.

DROP OUT OF CLASS

Now, let's jump into another model of ministry churches have promoted over the last several decades. If Sunday is the optimal day to get families to come to church, then it makes sense that Sunday is the most strategic time to teach kids the Bible. It's no wonder churches have traditionally reserved a segment of time on Sunday morning to do just that.

The Classroom Model

The classroom model, or what some people may refer to as Sunday school, was initially designed to teach kids the Bible every Sunday morning. For years, I (Reggie) promoted and built Sunday school programs in a number of churches. My experience convinced me that Sunday school was uniquely designed to teach and educate a child. In my denomination, Sunday school was usually under the direction of a "Minister of Education." (That's not to be confused with government leaders who determine the education policies in a number of countries. Although, the Minister of Education in our church did function like a Vice President to the Senior Pastor.)

The education strategy was simple.
Every age group had a class.
The curriculum was designed to teach
the Bible in a systematic way.
Individuals were arranged in classrooms with a
teacher who presented a weekly lesson.
Nobody could become a member until they
attended three consecutive weeks.
And everyone was evaluated by a weekly report.
(Cleverly designed envelopes recorded
attendance, tithe, Bible reading, etc.)

The plan was to design an hour each week to make sure kids who grew up in church were Biblically literate. (As we've already stated, the average kid who consistently attends church goes about 40 hours a year. When you contrast that with the 400 hours this year those same kids will study math, reading, and history, you realize it's quite a challenge.)

We created the following chart to illustrate the primary characteristics of a classroom model.

SUNDAY SCHOOL

Goal: Education
(That's why Sunday school was directed by a Minister of Education.)

Focus: Teach the Bible
(Kids lost points or were called out if they didn't bring one.)

Model: Classroom
(That's why teachers referred to it as "my class.")

Time: Sunday Morning
(That's why it was called "Sunday" school.)

Priority: Present the Lesson
(It was often read, unless someone creative used a flannel board.)

Volunteers: Recruit Teachers
(They were the most crucial and celebrated volunteers in ministry.)

Evaluation: Church Practices
(Leaders record each child's weekly attendance, Bible reading, tithe, etc.)

Emphasis: Learning Scripture
(It involved lots of Bible quizzes, Bible drills, and memory verse games.)

Before I continue, I want to acknowledge a lot of people owe their faith to committed Sunday school teachers who taught them weekly Bible stories. It has been a meaningful tradition within some denominations for over a century. I'm personally convinced that in the past, it had an important role in shaping someone's understanding of the Bible. It worked at a time when families spent most of their day working together, and local communities were characterized by common faith and values.

The truth is: I'm a Sunday school dropout. I hate to admit it, but I never enjoyed traditional Sunday school. When I went to church as a kid with my family, I'd pretend to go to my class and then sneak back outside to hide in the car until Sunday school was over. Maybe that's why I've actually spent most of my life trying to help leaders stop doing Sunday school. (Or at least to discontinue a style of Sunday school where kids sit in a room and listen to someone teach a lesson.)

We could go into some detail here on the history of Sunday school, and how it was originally started in the late 1700s in England to educate children who had to work in factories six days a week. But beyond that historical tradition, many leaders believe this model isn't the best way to disciple kids. Besides, shouldn't the name "Sunday school" bother us a little? Do we really think kids love school so much they want to go there on Sunday, too?

Many churches are recognizing the need to shift away from the idea of traditional Sunday school. Many ministries have decided to embrace a more relational model, while other churches are still wrestling with how to redefine Sunday school. In some cases they just change the name, but keep following a model that's losing ground.

One of the problems is simply that too many churches still expect a generation to embrace an outdated idea. If you Google

"Sunday school," you'll still find leaders who are defending and championing the concept as if the model is actually found in the book of Acts. Even those leaders will usually admit that the influence of Sunday school has been steadily declining for decades.

So, what if there isn't going to be a Sunday school revival? What if you can do **something better** than Sunday school? What if it's just time to let go and move on?

Photography is one of my hobbies, and I know a bunch of photographers who lost their business several years ago because they refused to go digital. Why? Because they loved film. Is anything wrong with film? Not at all! Photos made from film have a unique character and beauty unmatched by the average digital image. There will always be those who are advocates for film and may even become famous because of their work with film. But most photographers won't stay with film for one simple reason: People want digital images. They don't use film, and they keep very few prints. This generation uses smartphones to take selfies. So, most professionals are competing with people who carry a camera in their pocket and can upload the pic they just took to Instagram in seconds.

Film and digital images are simply methods. But the art of photography is timeless. Whenever we allow a method that worked for a season to trump something timeless, we make a grave mistake. Never sacrifice the next generation on the altar of your past methods or preferences.

Now if you happen to love Sunday school, I won't judge you— but you must at least admit Sunday school is not for everyone. Actually, it's not for most people. I can back that up with statistics. According to most research, nearly 75 percent of the people in the average community won't go to church this next Sunday. And less than half of those who go to church will go to Sunday school.

That means half the people who actually go to church don't even like Sunday school. Most people don't get up on Sunday morning and say, "I can't wait to go to a building, sit in class, and listen to someone teach me the Bible."

Sometimes we forget that we can't ultimately make kids go to church, learn the Bible, and follow Jesus. The sobering reality is that, sooner or later, kids will grow into teenagers who will drive themselves wherever they want to go on Sunday—just like every other day of the week. So, the only thing we can consistently and predictably do is to create an environment where kids or teenagers want to show up.

Smart leaders know that just because something worked once, doesn't mean it still works. It has becoming increasingly difficult to ignore the decades of evidence that most kids grow up and grow out of a classroom model. That's why it's strange that even in recent years, curriculums have been developed and volunteers retrained to launch new and improved versions of a class approach.

Several years ago, I heard Dr. Howard Hendricks, who was a seminary professor at Dallas Theological Seminary, speak about change. He said he had been invited as a consultant to critique a specific church. After observing everything that happened in their church on Sunday and during the week, he gave this report: "Unless you make some radical changes, you should just put up ropes at the front door, and charge people admission to see what church looked like 50 years ago." Dr. Hendricks was 70-plus-years-old at the time. I'm sure he had seen enough recent church history to give credibility to his observation. I also suspect many of that church's staff were surprised at his response. When you've been doing something the same way for a long time, it's easy to assume it's the best way to do things—especially when it works for the people who are coming. That's the reason a lot of churches will fight to defend a Sunday morning model. They mistakenly justify what they're doing because of the people who are coming, when they should consider evaluating what they're doing based on the people who *aren't yet* coming.

When it comes to creating a place for kids and teenagers, it's critical to re-evaluate and rethink your model frequently. You need to ask some hard questions related to what drives your strategy. The traditional values and practices behind most classroom models have existed for so long, they can make it hard to transition to more relational models.

When I was a young, idealistic student pastor in my first church, the teenagers complained that Sunday school was boring. So, I did what I thought was creative at the time. I stopped ordering the denominational literature, bought a book by Chuck Swindoll on understanding the Bible, redesigned the large group experience, and divided teenagers into smaller groups with leaders to have meaningful discussions. Within the first month I got a phone call from the chairman of deacons. His opening remark made me nervous: "My son told me you're no longer using the denominational quarterlies. Why is that?" I thought my reply was extremely logical: "Well, a lot of the teenagers say the denomination material is really boring, so I wanted to try something new." I will never forget how he responded: "What does boring have to do with anything? That's what we used when I was his age and look how I turned out." Soon after, I got a visit from the curriculum developers in our denomination asking me to explain my frustration with their content. It was then I learned how difficult it is to change anything that has existed in a church culture for decades.

There are a lot of incredible things someone can learn from a classroom model.

- It's important for kids and teenagers to memorize and apply core truths of Scripture.
- Gifted teachers should be recruited to communicate to kids.
- Kids should learn to navigate the overarching story of the Bible.

But we should also recognize that educating Christians is not the same thing as making disciples. We aren't claiming Sunday school was never effective. We are suggesting, however, that there are better models to disciple kids in today's culture. That's why we advocate designing a model that makes relationships a priority. Everyone can define or redefine any model in their ministry to be more relational (even Sunday school). But you have to be careful that you don't put new wine in old wineskins. You need to recognize the part of your system that needs to fundamentally change before you can move on. Consider the contrast that potentially exists between a model built around relationships and a model driven to educate kids.

	SUNDAY SCHOOL	SMALL GROUPS
Goal:	Education	Spiritual Formation
Focus:	Teach Bible	Make Disciples
Model:	Classroom	Circles
Time:	Sunday Morning	When It Works Best
Priority:	Present Lesson	Dialogue and Community
Volunteers:	Recruit Teachers	Develop Leaders
Evaluation:	Church Practices	Personal Faith
Emphasis:	Knowing Scripture	Knowing God

This chart is important primarily because many churches which try to shift to a group mindset are still driven by the primary goal to educate children and teenagers.

Are we saying every Sunday school model is focused on education and not spiritual formation? No. There are always exceptions. But educating Christians tends to be the default goal of most Sunday school programs.

Are we suggesting a small group ministry should not teach the Bible? Clearly, that's not the case. As we've explained in previous chapters, we think you can actually teach Scripture *more effectively* through caring, consistent SGLs who are personally involved with the kids they lead.

There are fundamental differences between the mindset that drives a Sunday school model and the mindset that drives a small group model. So if you're transitioning to a small group culture, remember the goal is to stimulate spiritual formation, not just teach spiritual information. There's a tendency for leaders who have been involved in Sunday school to default back to a classroom model simply because it's easier to recruit a few teachers than a host of small group leaders.

We have never claimed a small group model is easy. We just think it's worth it.

Remember this:
You don't *teach* kids to be disciples, you *lead* them to be disciples. So, maybe kids need more leaders, not more lessons.

TRANSITION TO CIRCLES

Shifting a culture takes time. It requires effort, planning, and a lot of conversations. You may experience setbacks. You'll probably face a bit of opposition. And chances are, it will take longer than you think.

We can't tell you exactly how long it will take to make this transition in your church. The amount of time required to move to a lead small approach will be affected by a number of variables including:

The history or age of your church.
The length of time you've been a leader at your church.
The traditions or style of your church.
The size or location of your church.

We've worked with leaders who feel they shifted the culture of their church within a few months, and others who feel it took a few years. A good rule of thumb is that it will probably take at least two years before your staff begins to feel like small groups are becoming a priority in your culture. Why is that? Because there's something about doing it the third time that begins to cement the value into the minds and hearts of your volunteers.

The first year, it feels like you're experimenting with a new idea.
The second year, it feels like you're improving
what you learned the first year.
The third year, it feels like you're establishing a pattern or model.

There's nothing magical about a two-year mark. It's just important to realize creating a culture where everyone champions the same priorities takes time. Therefore, we've organized the transition process into three major stages to help leaders understand what's involved in transitioning a culture. Remember, the suggested time frames are only guidelines depending on your church.

In **STAGE ONE** of your transition to a small group culture, you'll need to focus on gathering and sharing **INFORMATION**. This could take around six months.

In **STAGE TWO** of the transition, you'll begin **IMPLEMENTING** what you learned in the information phase. This could take another six months to a year.

In **STAGE THREE** of the transition, you'll need to continue **IMPROVING** your culture. This initial process of fine-tuning will likely take another six months, but it's something you should never stop doing. Creating a culture is one thing, but sustaining it is another. As a ministry leader, you'll never stop improving your culture.

Your goal, by the way, is **INTEGRATION**. It's what happens when the vision we've cast throughout this book becomes a reality. The goal is a church where groups are the answer for discipleship in every age group. It's a church where your structure supports groups, your leaders are empowered, and you've created better small group experiences. It's a place where every kid can belong.

When I (Reggie) wrote the book *Think Orange,* I worked with Carey Nieuwhof to outline a seven-step process for developing an integrated model of family ministry. They are the seven steps a church needs to take in order to move from where they are to where they want to be. We think these seven steps will work in moving to a small group culture, too, which is why we've included them as a part of the three stages of transition.

So if you're ready to . . .
drop out of class
do more than a concert
and go in circles,
then you're ready to begin
creating a culture where
relationships matter.

STAGE ONE: INFORMATION
(may take up to six months)

1. DO YOUR HOMEWORK.

If you're just beginning to take steps toward transitioning your church, this is likely where you are now. This book is a great start. Now, continue learning, asking questions, and considering what a small group culture might look like for your church.

Put this book, or another resource like it, into the hands of your core team so you can spark more conversations. Let these resources begin to craft a language around this issue so your team can discover and dream together. Identify a handful of ministries, comparable to yours in size or context, which have made the transition to a groups-based model, and learn from them.

Not sure where to find those leaders? Hop on your favorite social media platform and check out hashtags like

#thinkorange. You'll find a large, diverse community of leaders who passionately believe small groups are the answer and who'd love to have a conversation with you.

2. DEFINE AN ACTION PLAN.

Once your research is done, you need to create a plan. When I (Reggie) helped write *7 Practices of Effective Ministry*, our first practice was *Clarify the Win*. This step in the process will help you define what success will look like in your environment. This is essential when defining your action plan. Every part of the plan should lead to the win you've clearly articulated. Be specific and implement the second habit we covered earlier in the book—*Think Steps, Not Programs*. Every part of the plan should be a step toward the win. Don't do all of this in isolation. The more you involve your team, the more buy-in they'll have and the more help you'll have.

After you've clearly defined your goals and benchmarks along the way, put deadlines on each one. It's so easy to get busy working "in" on our ministry we forget to step back and work "on" it. Deadlines will keep this progress on your mind and on your calendar.

3. ESTABLISH A COMMUNICATION PROCESS.

Communication needs to be an ongoing process if you're going to lead any kind of change in an organization. But your communication needs an additional level of intentionality after you and your team outline an action plan. There are three circles of people you need to consider.

First, discuss your plan with your core decision-makers: the people who report to you (hopefully they will have been involved in creating the plan), key team members at your level, and the people you report to. These conversations are invaluable for you. Not only will they help you refine the plan, they'll give you the chance to refine your presentation of your plan for your most crucial audience: your influencers. These are key volunteers and focus groups of parents. Provide opportunities to test your ideas in partnership with them while you invite their input. When that's done, you can begin sharing the vision and the plan with a larger crowd: the rest of your volunteers, parents and kids.

Language plays a major role in creating a culture. And that language will either support your culture or undermine it. So some of you may need to consider making some revisions where . . .

teachers become *small group leaders.*
classrooms become *groups.*
lesson plans become *discussion questions.*
their *class* becomes their *few.*

The words we speak fuel our beliefs, and our beliefs drive our behaviors. Taking the time to carefully craft language can make the difference in your leaders and volunteers understanding your vision. It helps you fight the mentality that volunteers are "babysitters," and instead vital parts of the ministry strategy.

STAGE TWO: IMPLEMENTATION
(six months to one year)

4. REORGANIZE YOUR RESOURCES.

Now is the time for action. Begin reassigning your staff, budget, programs, volunteers, and resources to support small groups. It's possible you'll need to add something or someone to your structure, but it's also likely you'll need to redefine, reallocate, and subtract.

Remember, you may need to stop doing
some things that are successful if you want
to make groups *more* successful.

There may even be a few people who will opt to leave rather
than make the transition with you. That's okay. Acknowledge
and celebrate the success of where your ministry has been,
but stay focused on where you want to go. Patiently and
consistently remind people where you're headed and why.

5. DEVELOP A TRAINING STRATEGY.

A strategy is only as effective as the people who implement
it. You can have the greatest plan ever designed, and if the
staff and volunteer leaders in your ministry aren't prepared
to implement it, it will fail. Developing your leaders isn't
important, it's essential. Some people are natural-born
developers, and some aren't. If you aren't a "people developer,"
then find someone who is (even if they're a volunteer
themselves), and task them with the responsibility.

This is especially crucial when you're transitioning a group
of leaders from one strategy to another. They'll be working
against muscle memory from the old system and need
development all the more. Don't forget the vital role of vision in
this process. How we do what we do is important, but *why* we
do it will fuel the team during this tough season.

6. PROMOTE EVERYWHERE.

Have you ever watched the police or a utility service try to
change the direction of a lane of traffic? Flashing lights, men in
bright orange vests, and multitudes of signs all saying the same
thing and pointing in the same direction.

That's promotion. One sign or announcement won't do it.

A great plan comprised of memorable language has to be repeated and repeated. One stream won't work either; you need them all—social media, direct mail, sermon series, and, yes, announcements in the service. One of the most impactful ways to communicate a vision is to illustrate it through a story. A story of life-change your new strategy helped foster. Spread the word, and watch your vision spread along with it.

7. LAUNCH WELL.

Some leaders launch too quickly, before the vision for groups has spread or before the structure exists to support them. Others think and plan for years, but never launch. You aren't that leader. Launch well.

STAGE THREE: IMPROVEMENT
(six months to forever)

Shortly after your launch, you'll see areas that need improvement. You might see them *minutes* after your first week when well-meaning and critically constructive leaders start giving you feedback.

Every structure needs to be improved. Your leaders will always need more training. Your small group experiences will never stop needing some adjustments. So, if you get some of that critical feedback, that's okay. It's part of the process. Keep improving, keep tweaking, keep making things better.

Spotlight best practices you see your small group leader implementing on their own. Collect as many as you can, and each month blast them out on social media, emails, and your SGL meetings.

We love what Sue Miller did at Willow Creek Community Church. She said, "It took me three years to make the transition. We did it one grade at a time, beginning with the oldest kids. We let that group become a pilot group for the others and we bragged on them endlessly so other groups would get excited about following in their footsteps."

This transition will take some prioritization. Not every thing you want to change will carry equal weight. Gina McClain told us that when she started their small group transition what they really needed were storytellers. "But we knew we needed small group leaders more," she said. "So for six months, we put off our storyteller recruitment, used videos instead of live communicators, and focused instead on recruiting new small group leaders."

Remember that this will look different for every context. In every church your action plan will look different. Jenny Zimmer told us that her transition was gradual. "When I took my job, there was very little consistency with our volunteers. The idea of finding SGLs to serve every week for every kid was more than I could even wrap my head around. So, we started by asking leaders to begin serving every *other* week with the same group of kids. Then we staggered volunteers so that, even though we couldn't yet give kids the same leader every week, we could at least give them two leaders who alternated weeks. Is that the dream? No. But, today, almost three years later, we have more leaders then ever who have bought into the vision and have *asked* to become every-week leaders. To get here, we had to be flexible in the beginning. We had to meet our volunteers where they were, and lead them to where we wanted them to go."

Creating relationships that matter is possible. We can't tell you exactly when it will happen, but it *will* happen if you never stop improving and working toward your goal.

THE GOAL: INTEGRATION

Here's something we always say: You won't always be able to see a culture change. You'll just realize it has.

Remember, unless you know what you're transitioning to, you may not really be transitioning. Ultimately, you don't just want to see a small group culture happen in the age-group ministry you happen to care about. If your church is going to become a place where every kid belongs, a lead small culture must exist in every age-group ministry in your church. So, we wanted to give you a snapshot of what an integrated small group culture looks like. (If you skimmed the rest of the book, this is your summary.)

From time to time, you may need to do a quick ministry inventory to evaluate your approach to leading small. Use these nine statements to catalyze discussion. Invite core leaders on your team to talk through each item, and grade yourself to see where you can improve.

IMPROVE THE STRUCTURE

1. _____ A designated leader and team meet regularly to coordinate the small group strategy.

2. _____ You evaluate and tweak your ministry programs so they're steps to groups.

3. _____ Your seasonal and weekly calendar complements what happens in the culture and at home.

EMPOWER THE LEADER

1. _____ The majority of your small group leaders have shifted to a weekly responsibility.

2. _____ You do something every week to thank, encourage, and equip your SGLs.

3. _____ There's a clear, ongoing strategy for how you recruit and apprentice SGLs.

CREATE THE EXPERIENCE

1. _____ Your resources and curriculum support SGLs with what they need this week.

2. _____ The physical space is designed and managed to help the small group win.

3. _____ Everyone understands how to evaluate small group relationships and the small group experience.

You will never be done improving your structure.
You will probably never have all the SGLs you need.
You can usually do something more to
improve your weekly experiences.

Maybe that's why it's harder—not easier—
to create relationships that matter.
It will be messy, because relationships are messy.
People are messy.

Someone will probably get mad.

It will take longer than you think.

And you will never be done.

But it will be worth it.

Why will it be worth it?

Because kids need to be known.

Every kid needs to be known before they can feel welcome.

Every kid needs to be known before they can feel forgiven.

Every kid needs to be known before they can know they belong.

AUTHORS

REGGIE JOINER

Since someone on this writing team needed a little "experience," we thought maybe this was a good selection. Reggie Joiner is the founder and CEO of Orange, a non-profit organization whose purpose is to influence those who influence the next generation. Orange (ThinkOrange.com) provides resources and training for churches and organizations that create environments for parents, kids, and teenagers.

Prior to Orange, Joiner co-founded North Point Community Church in Alpharetta, Georgia, with Andy Stanley. During his 11 years as the Executive Director of Family Ministry, he developed a new concept for relevant ministry for children, teenagers, and married adults. If you end up road tripping with him across the country on Orange Tour, be prepared to stop at every antique store along the way. He has found a way to wear orange for 4,773 days and counting.

Reggie has authored and co-authored books including, *Think Orange, Seven Practices of Effective Ministry, Parenting Beyond Your Capacity, Lead Small,* It's *Just a Phase, New Kind of Leader,* and *Don't Miss It.* He and his wife Debbie live north of Atlanta and have four children, four grandchildren, and five granddogs. For more information about Reggie Joiner, visit ReggieJoiner.com or follow him on Instagram @ReggieJoiner.

KRISTEN IVY

It's hard to talk about small groups without getting some input from a small group leader. (Have you ever noticed how some small group leaders have opinions about how small groups should work?) Kristen has 15 years of experience leading small groups of middle school and high school girls. Her opinions about creating a small group culture come from years of reflecting on what ministry leaders can do to help the small group experience win. Ivy is Executive Director of Messaging at Orange. Before beginning her career at the company in 2006, she was a high school biology and English teacher, where she learned first-hand the joy and importance of influencing the next generation. She received her Master of Divinity in 2009. At Orange, Ivy has played an integral role in the evolution of the preschool, elementary, and high school curriculum, and has shared her experiences at speaking events across the country. Ivy is co-author of It's *Just a Phase* and *Don't Miss It.* She is a collegiate-cheerleading-captain-turned-theologian whose dream is to star in Cirque du Soleil.

Ivy lives in Cumming, Georgia, with her husband Matt, and her three children, Sawyer, Hensley, and Raleigh. For more information about Kristen Ivy, visit KristenIvy.com or follow her on Instagram @_Kristen_Ivy.

TOM SCHEFCHUNAS

Tom (or as most call him, Shef) has worked with students and adult leaders for over 20 years. He has been a teacher, coach, high school principal, student pastor, and father. He has a passion for recruiting and developing small group leaders, which is a big reason why he co-wrote the book *Lead Small* with Reggie Joiner. Shef has a degree in Physics and Education from Grove City College, a Masters in Educational Leadership from Georgia State, and a Masters in Biblical Studies from Dallas Theological Seminary.

Shef was the Multi-Campus Director of Middle School at North Point for 13 years where he poured into hundreds of volunteers and leaders at five campuses. For four years, Shef led the Student Initiatives at Orange, and is now leading Youth Specialties, a 50 year old organization committed to encouraging, equipping, and providing community for youth leaders. His passions involve working with, developing, and consulting volunteer and professional church leaders all over the world.

He and his wife Julie have three kids, and they swim and bike their way all over Georgia. Follow him on Instagram @coachshef.

THINK ORANGE

Two combined influences can make a greater impact than just two influences.

When you think Orange, you rethink the way you do ministry for kids and teenagers.

Find it at **OrangeStore.org**

WEEKLY

A Weekly Digital Strategy to Train Volunteers and Engage Parents

You want to engage parents and volunteers every week because you want parents and volunteers to engage kids every week.

But life is busy (and that's not all you do)
so we're here to help with . . .
// Customizable E-mails
// Easy-to-use Social Media Plans
// Editable Resources

Learn more at **GoWeekly.com**